A Guide to Appraisal Valuation Modeling

Readers of this book may be interested in these related publications available from the Appraisal Institute:

- *The Appraisal of Real Estate,* eleventh edition
- *Appraising Residential Properties,* third edition
- *The Dictionary of Real Estate Appraisal,* third edition
- *GIS in Real Estate: Integrating, Analyzing, and Presenting Locational Information,* Gilbert H. Castle III, editor
- *Mathematics for Real Estate Appraisers* by Clifford E. Fisher, Jr., MAI

A Guide to Appraisal Valuation Modeling

Mark R. Linne, MAI, CAE • M. Steven Kane • George Dell, MAI, SRA

**APPRAISAL
INSTITUTE®**

Reviewers: Gene Dilmore, MAI, SRA
Jeffrey A. Johnson, MAI
Michael MaRous, MAI, SRA

*Vice President, Educational Programs
and Publications:* Larisa Phillips
*Director, Content Development &
Quality Assurance:* Margo Wright
Manager, Book Development: Stephanie Shea-Joyce
Editor: Michael McKinley
Book Design/Production: Michael Landis

For Educational Purposes Only

The material presented in this text has been reviewed by members of the Appraisal Institute, but the opinions and procedures set forth by the author are not necessarily endorsed as the only methodology consistent with proper appraisal practice. While a great deal of care has been taken to provide accurate and current information, neither the Appraisal Institute nor its editors and staff assume responsibility for the accuracy of the data contained herein. Further, the general principles and conclusions presented in this text are subject to local, state, and federal laws and regulations, court cases, and any revisions of the same. This publication is sold for educational purposes with the understanding that the publisher is not engaged in rendering legal, accounting, or other professional service.

Nondiscrimination Policy

The Appraisal Institute advocates equal opportunity and nondiscrimination in the appraisal profession and conducts its activities in accordance with applicable federal, state, and local laws.

Library of Congress Cataloging-in-Publication Data
Linne, Mark R.
   A guide to appraisal valuation modeling / by Mark R. Linne, M. Steven Kane, George Dell.
      p. cm.
   Includes bibliographical references and index.
   ISBN 0-922154-59-7
      1. Real property—Valuation—Econometric models. 2. Valuation—Statistical methods. I. Kane, M. Steven. II. Dell, George. III. Title.

HD1387 .L553 2000
333.33's—dc21   00-038583

Table of Contents

2.8 1,256.32 11,200.36
2.6 1,450.35 12,315.09
1.9 1,097.06 14,365.25
3.0 1,250.77 11,256.89

Foreword

2.8	1,256.32	11,200.36
2.6	1,450.35	12,315.09
1.9	1,097.06	14,365.25
3.0	1,250.77	11,256.89

Many appraisers see automated valuation models as a direct threat to their livelihood. Automation of the appraisal process expedites the underwriting process and is an attractive option for lenders, who have traditionally been appraisers' largest clients. In our increasingly competitive marketplace, data sources are proliferating wildly and appraisers must be ready to face the evolution of information technology. This challenge also presents savvy practitioners with an opportunity to take advantage of the strengths of AVMs and increase their efficiency and productivity, lower their overhead, and, above all, manage change.

A Guide to Appraisal Valuation Modeling will introduce skeptics to the mathematical modeling of market behavior. The handbook provides historical perspectives, statistical fundamentals, support for assertions of causality in appraisal reports, and the basics of regression analysis and model construction. Many of these topics are brought together in a case study on the valuation of lots in an actual residential subdivision. Throughout the text the authors highlight the interplay of evolving statistical theory, traditional appraisal standards and practices, and simple common sense.

This timely publication is essential reading for any appraiser who has stubbornly resisted the encroachment of the number-crunchers. No matter how much you hated statistics in college, you can understand regression analysis. As the authors illustrate, most appraisers have been using similar statistical applications for years. With the basic information in this guide and a few technical refinements, you can use your existing knowledge to turn AVMs from an enemy to be feared into a trusted ally.

Woodward Hanson, MAI
2000 President
Appraisal Institute

Preface

2.8	1,256.32	11,200.36
2.6	1,450.35	12,315.09
1.9	1,097.06	14,365.25
3.0	1,250.77	11,256.89

There has long existed a dichotomy within the appraisal profession: essentially the partitioning of the appraisal worldview between mass appraisal and single-property appraisal. Both disciplines, to some extent, have been myopic with respect to the techniques and perspectives of the other. In many ways, this partitioning inhibits the transference of knowledge between the two. Assessment practitioners, charged with the simultaneous valuation of thousands of commercial and residential properties, have had to develop perspectives and techniques that enable them to process myriad data points into a reasonable and defensible framework. Conversely, fee appraisers have traditionally focused on fewer data points to develop their estimates of value. There is clear evidence that the roles of the two disciplines are rapidly converging with the integration of statistical techniques and data availability.

Assessment practitioners were among the very first to realize the benefits and potentials of technology, and the first to embrace it, as much out of necessity as desire. Technology became the bridging mechanism, allowing for the timely and accurate valuation of the assessment database, often totaling hundreds of thousands of properties. Assessment practitioners made significant advances in computer-assisted mass appraisal (CAMA) in the 1970s and 1980s, technologies that are now referred to in the field as *automated valuation models,* and they continue to be leaders in the field through innovative and ever more accurate valuation methodologies. In addition, they have also made significant advances in other related areas such as public databases and cadastral mapping/GIS.

The need for mass appraisal techniques in the private sector has never been more prevalent. Current uses range from instantaneous property valuations for lending purposes to portfolio valuations for asset management.

In many ways, this book is the result of the movement of ideas from the mass appraisal field to fee appraisal as well. Two of the authors began in the assessment field and later moved into fee appraisal. In so doing, they began to realize how few of the techniques they were familiar with were used in the private side of appraisal. Indeed, mass appraisal techniques were generally derided by fee appraisers. A perspective that examined data from an aggregation of sales, in contrast to the mere examination of a handful of sales, was a view that was generally dismissed rather than embraced.

Gradually, as the importance of statistics began to enter the mainstream to a greater extent, they began to use these techniques in their day-to-day practice, with the understanding that the techniques they employed had a practical application and appropriateness that provided a greater understanding of the appraisal process. Over time, the practice of incorporating statistical analysis techniques into the fee appraisal process became more widespread as statistical data became more readily available. With data now available in abundant quantity, the ability to accurately interpret statistical data has become paramount. Appraisers today must become more aware of the availability and meaning of data.

While mass appraisal continued to develop these highly specialized systems, a group of generalists were also in the midst of converting from arguments expressed in words to logic built on mathematics—a logic that recognizes the stochastic nature of all data and the probabilistic nature of all such results. These generalists are today's applied economists.

The field of economics was similarly impacted strongly by the power, availability, and low cost of computers. While computers began to be found in economics departments at most universities in the late 1960s, their real day came with the arrival of the desktop computer. The concurrent development of applicable statistical and mathematical software and the improvement of data quality and availability created an explosive growth of the scientific method into all the social sciences.

Today, the study of econometrics is of fundamental importance to business administration students, and is employed by applied economists, accountants, geographers, marketers, engineers, medical researchers, and political interests.

A major challenge of this book has been to integrate the diverse set of terminology employed by the various users. In particular, we have attempted to use and resolve similar words from the fields of mass appraisal, traditional appraisal, and economics. Mass appraisal appears to have developed a small but specialized terminology, otherwise adopting the most current economics vocabulary. Traditional appraisal, contrarily, grew as a cottage industry with some quaint word development. Wherever possible, we have attempted to favor the more general economic terminology. The very nature of this book has forced us to apply more rigorous language whenever possible. We have favored words that are more closely defined and more generally accepted by other disciplines outside just real estate appraisal.

Another advantage of this strategy is that we hope this book has some appeal to non-realty asset valuation solutions. Each of the numerous asset valuation branches, such as business, personal property, and intangibles, have a set of unique terminology. By favoring the more general terminology, we hope to help melt the barriers between these cousins, and show the universality of the econometric method. Concurrently, we make the users of appraisal reports and property analyses more able to understand similar processes across these asset types.

We are in the nexus of a transformational series of events: the significant synergism between the availability of computing power and the application of this power to the available database through the framework of statistical techniques and evaluative tools. By approaching this process with an open mind and with a desire to adapt and enhance the appraisal process, those who choose to adapt will be those who survive and thrive.

About the Authors

Mark R. Linne, MAI, CAE, has a varied background in appraisal. Mr. Linne is the Managing Director of Rocky Mountain Valuation Specialists, which specializes in complex residential and commercial appraisal issues throughout Colorado. He has been active in the development of adaptive valuation technologies including automated valuation models (AVMs) and was a member of the development team responsible for the creation of one of the first AVMs, capable of valuing over 750,000 residential properties along the Colorado Front Range. Mr. Linne has an extensive background in both appraisal and assessment, especially in areas melding the two disciplines. He serves as Vice Chairman of *The Appraisal Journal* Review Board and is a member of the Educational Publications and Communications Committees of the Appraisal Institute as well as serving on the Editorial Board of *Valuation Insights and Perspectives* magazine. Mr. Linne has been active in both writing and lecturing, and has authored numerous articles on statistical analysis and the future of appraising, including those for *Valuation Insights and Perspectives, Assessment Digest,* the *Colorado Real Estate Journal,* and others. Mr. Linne is one of only a handful of appraisers who hold both the MAI and the Certified Assessment Evaluator (CAE) designation of the International Association of Assessing Officers, where he has served on the Ad Hoc Committee on Computer-Assisted Appraisal.

M. Steven Kane has worked as a statistical analyst in fields as widely varying as criminal justice, biometrics, and real estate appraising. It is in this latter area of discipline that Mr. Kane has excelled. He was the chief appraisal valuation modeler for a residential AVM product developed in Colorado. This product was sold to and used by several major lending institutions in Colorado and continues to be used today. Mr. Kane is currently pursuing his designation from the

Appraisal Institute and is concurrently pursuing a Master's Degree in Real Estate Appraising from the University of St. Thomas. Mr. Kane is presently developing the valuation architecture for a general econometric model for Colorado's mountain resorts, which includes the Vail and Aspen markets. Mr. Kane began his career in appraising with the Denver Assessor's Office as a residential appraiser, working on both single-family and multifamily properties. His work in the criminal justice field included econometric analysis of court caseloads. His work in biometrics included work on a federally funded AIDS prevention project; his findings were published by the Centers for Disease Control, and he has appeared on "NBC Dateline" as part of this project. Mr. Kane has extensive experience on the lecture circuit and classroom in all three of these fields of analysis.

George Dell, MAI, SRA, is a practicing appraiser, teacher, and expert witness in Southern California. Educated in economics and business at San Diego State University, he saw the natural progression of economics from a "word art" form to scientific discipline, and the inevitable identical transition in the world of real estate analysis and appraisal. Mr. Dell has developed, written, and teaches several seminars and courses focused on the application of econometric principles to real estate appraisal. His work emphasizes the importance of established appraisal principles when integrating technological capability. His ability to place difficult concepts into familiar "case study" settings enables the rapid, practical learning of otherwise tedious statistical procedures. His practice emphasizes the viability of quantitative and graphic methods as analytical methods as well as presentation tools—whether for students, clients, or juries and judges. His experience as a motivational speaker brings an unusual enthusiasm to the important technical topics covered in this book. He has served in various capacities at local chapter, regional structure, and Appraisal Institute national committees and elective positions.

Acknowledgments

As with any undertaking, there are many who have inspired, contributed to the authors' thought processes, or provided valuable guidance at many junctures along the way. For the opportunities to work on automated valuation models and develop an understanding of the statistical applications, we thank Robert Deuschele and Daniel Shum of FirstBank Holding Company of Colorado, whose support enabled us to assist in the creation of a workable automated valuation model. We also wish to acknowledge Nathan Medvidovsky, whose early support and later efforts allowed us the freedom (however indirectly intentioned) to pursue the writing process more completely.

Our thanks to Thomas Motta and Christopher Bettin, whose initial enthusiasm became an important validation as we sought to bring the structure and order to our daily appraisal work necessary to devote the time to the completion of the manuscript, and who helped to compose the ideas that resulted in the finished text.

We are especially thankful for the hardworking members of the Educational Publications Committee, especially the committee chair, Mike MaRous, and the reviewers who provided the critical first reading of the text; their support and encouragement resulted in a better text. Staff members Stephanie Shea-Joyce and Michael McKinley were supportive throughout the editorial process, and their expertise is evidenced in the finished product.

George Dell would like to add his personal thanks to the numerous professors at San Diego State University and the University of California, San Diego, who contributed to this venture through their teachings and scholarship: George Babilot, Dan Steinberg, Raford Boddy, Eric Brunner, Camilla Kazimi, Douglas Stewart, David Macky, Duane Steffy, John Conlisk, Graham Elliot, Mark Machina, Joel Sobel, Ross Starr, Halbert White, Walter Heller, Richard T. Carson, and Vladimir Rotar.

Finally, we wish to thank our families for their patience over the last four years.

Chapter 1

Introduction and Overview

As the once glacial pace of technological advancement becomes an avalanche, every industry struggles to increase efficiency and reduce costs by adopting new, more powerful tools. Terms like *information overload* and *data smog* have been invented to give a name to the frustration and fear many professionals have about the glut of factoids, figures, and forecasts. "Easy" data can obscure the relevant information and discourage meaningful analysis.

Like other professionals in data-intensive fields, real estate appraisers and their clients today are faced with an overload of data and analytical techniques. Easy data benefit the appraiser but also create new challenges. To handle the massive amounts of property and economic data available from the Internet, government publications, and their own files, appraisers (and the users of appraisal services) need to know the answers to the following questions:

- How do I get concise answers from wide and deep sources?
- What are the steps?
- What do I need to learn?
- Why should I use one analytical procedure over another?

Appraisers need techniques to organize the data they collect in a cohesive but simple manner. Some clients are only interested in the final number. Others want market parameters and risk analysis. Still others will want an explanation of the entire analytical process. Users of appraisal services also need to understand how the available data are best used. Proper review of this new type of appraisal product will require new expertise.

The purpose of this book is to answer basic questions about the characteristics and uses of available data sets and, more importantly, how to analyze, interpret, and present that data effectively. Appraisers must understand how to use robust analytical techniques and understand their limitations. This is especially true when evaluating the output from pre-digested and pre-analyzed *automated valuation model* (AVM) products, either for an appraisal or as a consumer of such analysis services. The general rules of appraisal, as delineated in the Uniform Standards of Professional Appraisal Practice (USPAP), establish a minimal level of client confidence. Nevertheless, USPAP allows for and encourages the use of the most effective and reliable tools, techniques, and methods. USPAP does not limit the appraiser from the use of AVM and econometric tools. It simply assures that the product cannot be openly misleading, inappropriate, or carelessly generated.[1]

This handbook is not meant to replace a standard statistics textbook, which should be a fundamental reference. Nor will it replace an understanding of basic appraisal principles and practices. Rather, it should be seen as a supplement to such knowledge and a guide through specific issues and problems. To get the most out of this book, readers should

- Have access to a computer
- Have the ability to manipulate basic data sets (such as through a spreadsheet)
- Keep an open mind about the usefulness of statistical analysis in appraisal practice

The statistical analyses discussed in this book employ principles derived from mass appraisal practices and fundamental econometric modeling techniques. In the future, such analyses will become an integrated approach to value and/or augment one of the three traditional approaches to value. Appraisers, investors, underwriters, and litigators must become proficient in statistical analysis and extend their mathematical competence if they want to develop their more scientific skills as appraisers, analysts, and users of these services. Their future success will depend on it.

Threat or Opportunity—An Analogy

In the early 1990s, accounting and bookkeeping software allowed businessmen and -women to perform many functions that previously required the expertise of accountants. This software, which was originally perceived as a threat to the livelihood of accountants, is now an important tool of the profession, making accountants more productive, more accurate, and better able to focus on sophisticated analytical issues. A similar strategy is a blueprint for valuation professionals, who would be wise to apply the powerful tools of PC-based statistical analy-

---

1.   The Appraisal Standards Board has provided guidance for the use of automated valuation models by appraisers in Advisory Opinion 18. The numbered Standards and certain other portions of USPAP (e.g., the Competency Rule) also address the larger issue of the proper use of data and analytical tools in developing an opinion of value and reporting the result of an appraisal.

sis to appraisal and property economics. Those who are able to integrate the best elements of human judgment and computer technology will be the model of the appraisal profession in the next century, and users of such services who understand the techniques will possess sharper, more reliable decision-making abilities.

How to Use This Book

The discussion of statistical methods in this book will ultimately lead to the exploration of regression functions. Along the way readers will learn about techniques to describe collections of data (how big, how wide-ranging, patterns, and averages) and specific ways to measure differences between data (such as measuring external effects on one neighborhood by comparing it to a similar neighborhood).

This book builds to the linear regression process because a solid understanding of the fundamentals of data analysis provides a foundation for further investigation into more complex (but more reliable) procedures. Note that most real-world market phenomena taken at a point in time can best be explained as a matrix of linear relationships. The process of purchasing a home is often modeled mathematically as a linear event, where potential buyers add positive and negative factors for each buying option. Factors such as location, physical characteristics, and externalities influence buyers, who in turn shape the market. Statistical analysis recognizes the probabilistic, "iffy" nature of these factors and can help describe and relate these factors to value.

The examples in this handbook are primarily residential in nature but are equally—or more so—applicable to commercial property and portfolios that include real property. Amenity properties and income-producing properties are considered. Special-use properties, mixed-use properties and those with detrimental conditions or one-of-a-kind features can be modeled, also. Statistical analysis has been used in marketing products, determining consumer spending patterns, and areas where human behavior can be measured quantitatively (or qualitatively), with defined outcomes. Such analyses can be descriptive, inferential, or both; the differences between these two types of analyses will be explained further in this book. Descriptive data techniques, measures, and statistical tests can apply to both income-motivated and amenity-motivated property data analysis. While AVMs are commonly used for residential appraising, regression-based modeling has also been used in a limited way by commercial appraisers, especially commercial mass appraisers in county assessor's offices. The case study in Chapter 9 illustrates the use of regression techniques in the appraisal of a subdivision.

The use of automated valuation models is also addressed. Appraisers today may be asked to review and use software that purports to calculate property values *without* human assistance once the data have been entered into the computer. Clients with access to such products may need appraisers to explain, augment, or review their output. An appraiser must understand the basics of these valuation products to use them effectively and confidently. There are ways to integrate these fixed (or "adjustable") models into more accurate, more reliable conclusions.

One final note: many appraisers already use statistical techniques, particularly descriptive tools, in their analyses. They have demonstrated that these methods are appropriate and practical for the appraisal profession. To many professionals, the procedures described in this book will be familiar, although the array of possible applications may come as a surprise. What goes on inside the head of an appraiser is quite akin to statistical modeling—it has been called the *art of appraisal.*

Statistics embraces the probabilistic nature of human behavior, measurement, forecasting, and risk.

- It gives users measures of reliability and measures of accuracy.
- It builds on the underlying mathematical logic and rigor.
- It connects to economic knowledge and appraisal practices.

The three together—mathematics, statistics, and economics—combine to give appraisers more science, less art, and more quickly delivered.

Chapter 2

Historical Perspectives and the Use of Statistical Analysis

2.8	1,256.32	11,200.36
2.6	1,450.35	12,311.09
		25
3.0	1,250.77	11,256.89
2.5	1,332.18	10,325.02
15.60		9,385.00
2.3	1,220.09	14,200.72

Residential analysts face data overload at every level, from regional and neighborhood data downloaded from the Internet to large quantities of comparable sales data. Commercial appraisers also face problems of limited relevant comparable sales or lease data but strongly linked markets and numerous economic factors.

In the late 1980s, niche service providers, who collect data in an electronic medium, began to emerge in the marketplace. Collecting data from primary sources such as the local assessor's office or multiple listing service (or a combination of both) offered cost-effective alternatives to clients requiring such information.

Appraisers also have ready access to demographics, population dynamics, social and industry data, and input on virtually every factor in the supply and demand equation. The advent of the Internet has compounded this trend geometrically by allowing computers to reach beyond their own data sets and access data worldwide. Integration of "net" data into host-based analytical systems continues the convergence.

Mass Appraisal Versus Single-Property Appraisal

Mass appraisers have employed and refined data analysis skills for many years. Indeed, one important historical trend is the convergence of single-property appraisal and mass appraisal. The text *Property Appraisal and Assessment Administration* compares and contrasts the two disciplines as follows:

> Simply stated, single-property appraisal is the valuation of a particular property as of
> a given date; mass appraisal is the valuation of many properties as of a given date,

using standard procedures and statistical testing. Both require market research. The principal differences are in scale and quality control.[1]

In essence, valuation models developed for mass appraisal purposes must reflect supply and demand patterns for groups of properties rather than for a single property.

Valuation models attempt to perform several related functions:

- To predict, replicate, or explain the market value of properties from real estate data
- To represent the forces of supply and demand within particular markets
- To replicate one of the three theories of valuation—the cost approach, the sales comparison approach, or the income capitalization approach

Quality is measured differently in mass and single-property appraisal. In mass appraisal, statistical methods are used to measure deviations of all sales in the population database from their mass-appraised values. If *most* mass-appraised values for properties with sales fall within a predetermined average deviation from actual sale prices, the work quality is considered good. In single-property appraisal, quality has usually been judged by a direct comparison with a limited set of comparable sales. Single-property appraisal analyzes a fixed number of points, usually no more than three to five data points, while mass appraisal might analyze hundreds or even thousands of data points. These parameters, however, are now beginning to change on the fee appraising side.

A critical similarity between both mass and single-property appraisal is their adherence to fundamental principles of applied economic analysis. Each appraisal method is a logical, systematic effort to collect, analyze, and process data in a manner that produces a well-reasoned value opinion.

One important historical similarity is the use of professional standards to guide practitioners on both sides of the profession. To value single properties, fee appraisers have historically implemented standards that focus on sound applications of agreed-upon techniques. Mass appraisers have focused on appraisal techniques that emphasize the equitable valuation of a large group of properties, as mandated by the public scope of county assessor departments. Appraisal principles that focus on the use of statistical analysis, whether from a mass appraisal or fee appraisal perspective, are still developing.

Historical Basis

The Birth of AVMs

Today fee appraisers and institutional investors are commonly involved in discussions surrounding the applications of AVMs, multiple regression analysis, heuristic models, expert systems, and the like, all of which use statistics in some

---

1. Joseph K. Eckert, PhD, general editor, *Property Appraisal and Assessment Administration* (Chicago: International Association of Assessing Officers, 1990), 80.

fashion to predict value and to explain its nature. While most practicing appraisers only began to hear of these terms in the late 1990s, the discipline, as used by mass appraisers, has been around since the 1970s.

County assessors embraced technology as a means of addressing the need to value thousands and sometimes hundreds of thousands of properties, often with minimal staffing. To accomplish this seemingly impossible task, assessors employed computer-assisted mass appraisal (CAMA). Larger jurisdictions that could afford the costly technology found that they could effectively value properties with higher degrees of accuracy and then defend the values in a public forum initially leery of computer techniques.

Private sector companies that were examining the development of CAMA technology for lending institutions initially rejected the use of assessment data, insisting that the data were incorrect, inappropriate, and lacked the necessary specificity to meet private sector needs. That perception has now changed.

Private Sector Efforts

The private sector was slow to recognize advances in the assessment field until the early 1990s. Statistical analysis was applied only in limited cases; few appraisers had access to the large databases, and collecting, purchasing, or digitizing such databases was expensive. Furthermore, the fee appraising community and users had a lingering distrust of many assessment methodologies, particularly in the area of data classification. This distrust was not entirely unreasonable; the assessment community itself was aware that many data sets were missing data and contained errors. These issues were addressed during the 1990s. Assessment data, at least on an individual property basis, is now more available, some of it on the Internet. Assessment personnel have had years to verify and update data sets and today fee appraisers and assessment appraisers have developed a mutual respect for the valuation practices used in both disciplines.

Before the 1990s the widespread application of comparative property analysis, pioneered within the assessment community through the use of multiple regression analysis, was virtually unknown within the private sector, or it was limited to concepts such as matched pair analysis. Because the matched pair method could only solve for one variable or differential at a time, the analysis required two properties that were identical in all respects but one and that ignored variability—requirements that limit its questionable usefulness.

The application of comparable sales adjustments, a primary tool for fee appraisers, was developed based on the available scope of data, which was often limited to less than 10 comparable sales. To take advantage of the larger data sets available today, appraisers have had to develop a wider range of analytical techniques.

Despite the current affectation for chic valuation techniques (e.g., neural networks and artificial intelligence), all of these techniques essentially employ standard appraisal methodology on a mass appraisal scale, using updated versions of the computer-assisted modeling that had been under development and in use since the 1970s and even earlier.

Complications of Automation

One problem currently being explored by those within and outside of the appraisal profession is the excessive reliance placed on purely statistical solutions to the question of value. The emphasis on statistical models and a statistical solution has created a rift between statistical models and real estate valuation models. Many of the products currently offered to lenders rely too heavily on statistical analysis without incorporating the requisite appraisal judgment. Indeed, without a sufficient background and underlying basic knowledge of the appraisal process, these products sometimes do not model what they purport to model. The appraiser and user must consider the applicability question to evaluate the conclusions of such models.

In many respects, statistical applications are necessary to account for multiple differentials of property characteristics. By ignoring statistics, appraisers risk abdicating this aspect of analysis to statisticians, accountants, opposing expert witnesses, or even bank tellers.

The next section summarizes the evolution of automated valuation models and traditional appraisal practices. Two consequences are clear:

1. The market needs a more rational, objective, scientific basis on which to make decisions, performed by professional individuals competent both in appraisal theory and practice and in computerized data analysis and reporting.
2. Appraisers must gain competence in statistical analysis and begin using more "pictures" and fewer words.

The result will be the most efficient *econometric* blend of economic (appraisal) theory and statistical analysis, on the foundation of mathematical relationships.

Appraisal Valuation Modeling

This heading, and the title of this book, may be a triple redundancy. An appraisal is a valuation. The valuation process is a model. What we are talking about here are electronically assisted models that go beyond spreadsheets and words. We are talking about models that rely on underlying economic theory, using mathematical relationships, analyzed *and presented* in the scientific language of statistics. Those statistics recognize, expose, and measure the probabilistic nature of human preference as well as business decision making.

While *product* technologies continue to impact valuation professionals and users, the greatest impact on the profession will be from *process* technology. Process technology incorporates the full production continuum from electronic data availability to electronic delivery of reports. In between there is

1. Data improvement, enhancement, clarification, and verification
2. Analysis (without data truncation)
3. Interpretation (including reliability opinion)
4. Presentation

Figure 2.1 illustrates the evolution of the process technology continuum.

Figure 2.1	Evolution of Process Technology			
	Traditional Appraisal Model	**Econometric Appraisal Model**	**Adjustable AVM**	**Fixed AVM**
Data selection	Three to five best comps	*All* comps in the chosen market area	Comp choice may be modified by the operator	Comps chosen by internal algorithm
Criteria for data inclusion	Availability, appraiser experience, time truncation	In the market area and in the market segment; time weight/adjust	Operator decision or a modifiable simple algorithm	Algorithm, spatial, or area comparability decision tree
Analysis process (adjustment)	Appraiser experience or market support	Statistical support for appraisal process	Operator support for the statistical process	Fixed, expert system, or neural network
Reliability	Depends on appraiser experience, education in traditional methods	Depends on appraiser competence in data analysis methods	Depends on quality of AVM and *appraisal* competence of the AVM operator	Depends on the quality, applicability of the AVM
Bias	Inadvertent or intentional bias	Assumptions are clear, reproducible analysis	Assumptions may be concealed, but analysis is reproducible	Algorithm is secret, applicability bias, unique answer, or non-reproducible
Reliability, risk, or confidence rating	No	Yes, explicit	Explicit, but subject to operator judgment	Explicit, but subject to applicability error
Usefulness for unique or special-use properties	Good, depends on appraiser competence and data "ownership"	Excellent, integrates market knowledge and market analysis	Fair, will usually get in the way of reliable analysis	Poor
Licensing for FIRREA*	Yes	Yes	Yes	The applicability decision may be an appraisal act
Future prospects	Theory and practice are self-limiting	Embraces changes in technology and data analytical theory	Will continue to improve. Operator competence is the key	Will continue to improve; a general model is distant

* Financial Institutions Reform, Recovery and Enforcement Act, which mandates appraisal competence and licensing enforcement.

	2.8	1,256.32	11,200.36
	2.6	1,450.35	12,315.09
	1.9	1,097.06	14,365.25
	3.0	1,250.77	11,256.89
	2.5	1,332.18	10,325.02
	2.6	1,115.60	9,385.00
	2.3	1,220.09	14,200.72

Chapter 3 *Statistical Analysis and Data*

One of the purposes of this handbook is to dispel some of the prejudicial myths about statistical applications by demonstrating that appraisers can and should use statistical analysis in every appraisal. The fundamental concepts need to be embraced, not feared. This chapter will focus on general concepts and applications of appraisal-oriented statistical analysis. The following chapters will describe in detail how and when to apply several useful and powerful but simple statistical methods.

The Scope of Analysis

Statistical analysis gives one the ability to 1) identify, 2) measure, and 3) interpret *events* in nature. These *events*, or *phenomena*, can be thought of as any measurable activity; in the case of real estate valuation, this activity involves human action, such as buying, selling, renting, or developing real property. Such phenomena are measured by monetary transactions or other quantitative indices, allowing the appraiser to categorize, gauge, and compare the activity.

What phenomena *cannot* be analyzed? Obvious examples include real estate activity of a confidential nature, where the data are concealed. In such cases, market- or industry-derived factors can be used, as long as the appraiser makes it clear in the appraisal that specific property data are unavailable. In a case where standard factors or comparable properties are not available, an appraiser may not be able to perform the appraisal assignment at all. However, some statistical techniques are available to deal with missing data.

Statistical Analysis in the Three Approaches to Value

Data analytic tools are not a separate approach but are usable throughout the valuation process. The *cost approach* looks at the construction costs of a given improvement on a given piece of land, with the land value estimated by some kind of separate analysis (usually sales comparison). Building costs often refer to cost indices provided by vendors such as Marshall and Swift, Dodge, and others. These indices themselves constitute a form of statistical compilation; that is, they are derived from the typical costs of construction, a form of averaging that statisticians call a *measure of central tendency*. Other factors such as time or location are used to modify the cost index values. All of these are statistical results. "Neighborhood" ranges, predominant values, vacancy rates, and land uses are forms of descriptive statistics. In many ways appraisers already use statistical analysis in the cost approach as well as in market, neighborhood, and economic condition descriptions.

The *income capitalization approach* also uses statistical analysis. Comparable rental properties are organized in an array and then analyzed to select the most competitive properties to determine a market rental rate. The process of selecting, adjusting, and reconciling these arrayed properties can be straightforward or complex. Many commercial appraisers use simple statistical analysis applications in their appraisal reports, from something as fundamental as the determination of an appropriate capitalization rate or gross rent multiplier to techniques as sophisticated as supporting elements within the discounted cash flow analysis.

Appraisers use much of the traditional statistical analysis in the third approach, *direct sales comparison*. The variable being measured is usually the value of the property. Sales comparison simply relates the prices of similar properties to the subject property either by a table/spreadsheet adjustment mechanism or qualitative comparison where selected properties are compared to the subject, one component at a time. The sales comparison approach also clearly illustrates the three applications of statistical analysis; that is, it helps the appraiser select comparable properties (identification), measure differences in property characteristics (measurement), and apply adjustment amounts (interpretation) to arrive at an estimate of value.

Components of Statistical Analysis

The following sections will examine the three components of statistic analysis in appraisal:

1. Identification
2. Quantification
3. Interpretation

The sales comparison approach is used as an example of such analyses.

Identification

The question of identifying what particular real estate phenomenon (or variable) is of interest depends on the purpose of the analysis. The goal could be one of the following:

- To specify important elements of comparison that control overall value
- To value a group of properties in a given area
- To create a broad valuation model
- To "mark to market" (value) a portfolio of real property, financial securities, or derivatives
- To estimate risk

The goal of the analysis often determines what type of modeling strategy should be employed. For example, an appraiser should not create a regression model with numerous variables to value residential properties if the market transaction that sets those values in the real world is limited to a smaller number of variables. The presence of a swimming pool may theoretically increase property value, but that increase can be affected by other factors, such as location (e.g., if the property is in Alaska or Arizona) or whether a pool is a typical upgrade feature. If there are no sales properties with swimming pools, then the appraiser cannot adequately analyze its impact on property values anyway. If most properties have swimming pools, like in wealthy areas in warmer climates, then it may be impossible to separate the impact that factor has because it is associated with all large, quality homes. *Identification*, therefore, is important not only in analyzing the overall valuation problem correctly but also in choosing the specific variables that will be analyzed.

Quantification

Once the relevant variables are identified (Step 1), measuring them and calculating their impact allows the appraiser to quantify their effect (Step 2). Calculating the influence of a phenomenon links the identification and interpretive steps.

The actual calculation of variable influence is often the easiest step in statistical analysis. This step can often take only a few seconds to complete using software such as electronic spreadsheets (Microsoft Excel, Lotus, Corel Quattro Pro) or databases (Access, dBase). Specialized analytical software, such as STATA, MATLAB, and SAAS, can often offer the best package for data analysis and is highly recommended. The analysis in this book uses SPSS (Statistical Package for the Social Sciences), but the reader can also use one of many other packages to perform similar analyses (at least the basic ones).

To correctly measure data the appraiser must understand:

- Some basic concepts behind data
- The types of data

- Limitations of the data
- Some considerations about the source of the data

Types of Data

Statisticians have developed several methods of classifying data types. The classic statistical data classification breaks down all data into the following groupings:

1. Nominal (qualitative)
2. Ordinal (qualitative)
3. Interval (quantitative)
4. Ratio (quantitative)

Figure 3.1	Examples of Four Types of Data		
Nominal data	Census tract		
	Type of building		
	Type of zoning	Qualitative	
Ordinal data	Quality		
	Condition		
	Utility		
Interval data	Time (years, months)		
Ratio data	Sale price		
	Size of building	Quantitative	
	Age of building		
	Size of parcel		
	Number of stories		

Nominal. Nominal variables signify membership in a particular group, with no quantifiable difference implied between the groups. In other words, a nominal variable simply *names* a phenomenon (*nominal* derives from the Latin root *nomen*, which means name). A generic example is a variable for fireplace, where properties possessing a fireplace have a value of 1 and those without a fireplace have a value of 0. There is no inherent numerical difference between these values; 0 and 1 are simply yes/no markers to distinguish between these two groups. Another example would be a location number, such as a subdivision number used by a county assessor's office. Each subdivision number is in effect a label that identifies that subdivision area uniquely.

Ordinal. An ordinal variable, where the value of the variable denotes a position within a ranking scheme, provides more information than a nominal variable but less than interval data. ("Ordinal" gives the "order.") A real-world example of ordinal data would be a school report card, where a grade of A is above B, which is in turn above a grade of C, and so on. Although the letter grade indicates the relative performance of the student within a recognized range of outcomes, ordinal data do not reveal any numeric differences between these ordered numbers—i.e., whether the school grading system is based on 90–100% for A and 80–90% for B, or on 90–100% for A and 60–90% for B, or some other scale. We know only that A is greater than B, and that both A and B are greater than C. We do not know the *magnitude* of difference between grades of A, B, and C.

An appraising example of this would be a qualitative scale, such as a measurement of the physical condition of the property. If the assessor's data file contains a four-level variable called *condition,* with 4 = excellent, 3 = good, 2 = average, and 1 = poor, the appraiser would still have some questions about the differences between these values. For example, how much better is a good property from an average property? Is the spacing between the rank categories consistent?

Assume that construction quality is included in a valuation model that allocates $5,000 to each increment of that characteristic based on differences between the average selling prices of homes. For example, properties with a rating of *excellent* would receive $20,000 ($5,000 × 4) while *average* properties would receive only $10,000 ($5,000 × 2). The actual sales data may show something entirely different, for example, where *excellent* properties were $25,000 above *good* properties, which in turn were only $3,000 above *average* properties. The scale simply does not reveal the difference in value between each condition level. This problem with spacing may be evident whenever there are more than two categories within the variable. Sometimes methods can be used such as paired sales analysis to create separate values for each quality level (and there are better ways to treat this problem using more advanced procedures such as regression analysis). Ordered data can be used as long as distance between variable values is not taken "as is."

Nominal and ordinal data are also known as *categorical data* because the primary information derived pertains to group membership (for example, if the property is part of Subdivision A or Subdivision B); these categories are either unranked (nominal) or ranked (ordinal).

Interval. For *quantitative data* (both interval and ratio data), the data value itself provides explicit information, in that equal differences have equal meaning. There is always a unit of measure involved, such as square feet, acres, roof pitch, or number of units. Most data of this type is *continuous,* in that it can always be measured more and more precisely, like square feet of area (e.g., 423.62... square feet). Or it can be *discrete,* like numbers of apartment units (1, 2, or 3) or number of baths (1, 1½, 2, 2½, etc.). With all quantitative data, either continuous or discrete, the intervals between the values are quantitatively meaningful.

Interval data allows adding and subtracting but not multiplying and dividing. For example, the difference between 2001 and 1998 is the same as between 1947 and 1945. However, there is no zero point, except in the Biblical sense. Another example is temperature, measured in Centigrade or Fahrenheit. These have an arbitrary zero, far above the real "absolute" zero. Ratios make no sense in this context—e.g., 50° F is not 10 times "hotter" than 5° F (how would you handle -5° F?).

Ratio. The other type of quantitative data, *ratio data,* does allow multiplication and division (as well as adding and subtracting). For example, a home that has 2,200 square feet of GLA is 83% larger than a home that has 1,200 square feet. The difference between the size of the two homes, 1,000 square feet, has real meaning that can be measured and interpreted as does the percentage difference (i.e., the difference in size divided by the size of the smaller house). On the other hand, a home with a quality rating of *excellent* and an ordinal value rating of 2 is not necessarily twice as valuable as a home with a quality rating of *average* that corresponds to a rating of 1.

The bottom-line difference between qualitative data and quantitative data is that the latter yields more information. Statistical analysis that uses interval or ratio data therefore yields more information.

Sources of Data

In real estate valuation, the necessary data can often be found in the files of the county assessor available to the public. Sales information can also be found in local MLS data downloads, the information source used by real estate brokers.

Integrating data from these sources has inherent challenges, such as ensuring the compatibility and consistency of variables across data sources. For example, how does each data source define gross living area (GLA)? If the county assessor defines living area as all above-grade, heated square footage while the MLS source considers living area as all above-grade square footage minus any heated porches or attics, then the analyst must decide which definition to use. In this case, one of the sources of data would have to be altered systematically to "fit" with the other source. This data editing process (also known as *filtering*) must be performed before data can be analyzed, and it requires an understanding of the nuances of both data sources.

Inconsistent definitions of house styles (split-level, bi-level, etc.) across different data sources are a common problem. For example, if the MLS data file considers living area associated with split-level style homes to include the garden-level area, while the assessor's data file groups the garden-level area with finished basement square footage, then a decision needs to be made as to a consistent definition for split-levels. (This can be even more problematic with bi-levels.) The example illustrated in Figure 3.2 is one of *inter*-definition inconsistency, where the definition of a certain variable for one data source does not agree with that of another source.

In the case of *intra*-definition inconsistency, definitions are not consistent within the same data source, for example, when one real estate agent's finished basement is another agent's garden-level component of total living area. Appraisers are always responsible for ensuring that public access data be consistent in their analyses when such data are used as part of their appraisal.

Figure 3.2 | **Same House, Different Definition of "Total Living Area"**

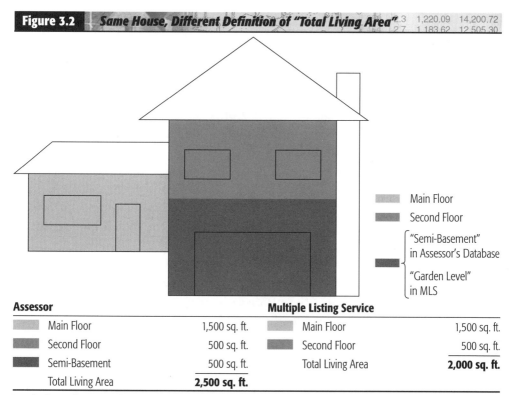

Assessor		Multiple Listing Service	
Main Floor	1,500 sq. ft.	Main Floor	1,500 sq. ft.
Second Floor	500 sq. ft.	Second Floor	500 sq. ft.
Semi-Basement	500 sq. ft.	Total Living Area	**2,000 sq. ft.**
Total Living Area	**2,500 sq. ft.**		

Note that the MLS does not consider "garden level" space part of the total living area.

Data Errors

Errors that create data problems are generally of two types. The first, *systematic error,* occurs when the data are consistently inaccurate or unreliable, a situation computer programmers describe with the phrase "garbage in, garbage out." Although the problem in this instance can be more pervasive within a data set, the correction of it can be fairly straightforward. For example, when verifying data collection and classification practices of the local assessor's office, an appraiser discovers that the assessors have been misclassifying finished basement area as part of total living area. The appraiser can then make adjustments by simply subtracting the finished basement area from total living area.

The second problem, *random error,* is less frequent but more difficult to identify and correct, specifically because the error occurs without an immediately recognizable pattern. This type of error can often be spotted when variable values are arrayed across several properties. For example, if a county appraiser makes an error in the living area of a particular property, the appraiser may find the error by comparing the same property with other properties in the same data file. The next step can be removing the property in question or exchanging the "bad" value with another value (sometimes referred to as a *proxy value*).

Strategies to get around both types of these "bad data" problems are illustrated in Chapter 7.

Interpretation

Once the data are identified and captured, choosing the type of analysis becomes the final analytical step. Some procedures simply illustrate the range of the data, either through descriptive means (frequency) or through index numbering (scores and rankings). In real estate, there are many examples of these types of measurements, such as average sale price or a ranking of the top-selling neighborhoods in a report. Here nominal and ordinal data can be used alongside interval data, such as neighborhood and sale price.

Procedures such as regression analysis can be used to compare many separate characteristics at once within a group of sale properties and then estimate their contributory weight to the value of the subject parcel. This ability to simultaneously compare many homes in a particular area gives the modern appraiser an analytical leg up over the traditional appraiser, so long as the market area has been properly identified and the data are properly prepared. In certain areas (e.g., custom home neighborhoods, mansion-dominated markets, mountain resorts, and areas crisscrossed with outside influences such as highways and boulevards), traditional appraisal methods remain superior to statistical methods that rely on a certain level of similarity (or homogeneity) between properties. In these cases, the statistical information may still yield valuable adjustment data for the appraiser. An example of this would be the use of a two-variable (one dependent, one independent) regression technique to derive the market impact of proximity to a highway that bisects a residential neighborhood.

Interpreting output from statistical analysis does not require the analyst to be a graduate-level statistician, as long as the steps outlined are followed. Fortunately, the appraiser or analyst has a large body of appraisal theory to judge the "soundness" of statistical output.

For example, if a regression-based valuation model yields an incremental value for fireplaces at $20,000 in a given neighborhood, the appraiser can compare that with other statistical information about this same area. If the average sale price is $350,000, then the appraiser may decide that the $20,000 per fireplace is a reasonable amount. On the other hand, if the average sale price is $80,000, then appraisal judgment may force the appraiser to reject this variable value as too extreme. Experience suggests that objective metric methods usually confirm traditional adjustment amounts.

In the latter case above, the fireplace variable may be masking another valuation factor not represented in the model (i.e., a "missing variable" problem). This masking can involve a related variable (such as a first-floor den) or another variable with no obvious direct relationship. For example, suppose five homes had one fireplace and five homes had two fireplaces. Also assume that the one-fireplace homes all sold early in the sale period, while all of the two-fireplace homes sold in the latter part of the sale period (the builder may have added the second fireplace as a market incentive). In this scenario, a portion of the fireplace value reported by the model could be reflecting sale price appreciation present in the market. This can be tested by looking at the market adjustment variable in the model: If the influence of changing market conditions was not reflected in the model or if it had a value that did not make sense (even a negative value), then the fireplace and market conditions variables could be identifying and measuring the same phenomenon. Statisticians call this situation *collinearity*, which means simply that two variables are interacting with one another in the analysis. (Collinearity will be covered in more detail in Chapter 8.)

Summary

In this chapter, some basics of statistical analysis were discussed. The purpose of statistical analysis is to identify, calculate, and interpret phenomena. In appraisal practice these events are often market transactions that help determine value in real property. To be studied, these transactions (and the variables involved) must be clearly defined and understood. The importance of appraisal knowledge and experience to the proper incorporation of statistical analysis in the appraisal process is clear—*appraisal theory, not statistical theory, always drives the process.*

Classifying, arranging, and just looking at data are key parts of statistical analysis. Data can "name," "order," or measure phenomena. Data can also be continuous, discrete (choice), or binomial (yes/no). Often certain nominal or ordinal data can be made to behave as interval/ratio data. Similarly, continuous data and discrete data can sometimes be "converted." How data are structured is a part of the analytical process.

Appraisers must be able to interpret whatever output is placed before them correctly, whether that output comes from a statistical software package, from an available statistician on duty, or from a canned AVM. Understanding the structure of statistical analysis is fundamental to analysts and users of appraisals. USPAP requires that the appraiser understand the data and analysis used in the appraisal process and to report that information in a manner that is credible and not misleading. For many readers, a report containing statistical output with confusing, complicated, or "black box" algorithms and unqualified conclusions can be misleading or just plain wrong.

2.8	1,256.32	11,200.36
2.6	1,450.35	12,315.09
1.9	1,097.06	14,365.25
3.0	1,250.77	11,256.89
2.5	1,332.18	10,325.02
2.6	1,115.60	9,385.00
2.3	1,220.09	14,200.72

Suppose an analyst wishes to include a section on sale price appreciation in an appraisal report. First the relevant data are described or summarized, such as the quarterly trend in the average sale price for residential homes in a given area. Then this trend is applied to the subject property. This may be as simple as applying a percentage factor to the subject property's concluded value.

Descriptive statistics simply do what their name implies, describe the patterns of data, e.g., by illustrating the distribution of sale prices or of home styles. Descriptive statistics are useful for visualizing the data (a form of analysis) and for presentation in a report (to help the reader visualize the data and understand the related conclusions). *Visual* (or graphic) descriptive statistics include bar charts, ogives, boxplots, and stem-and-leaf and scatter plots, among others. *Mathematical* (or summary) descriptive statistics include concepts about the group of data, such as

1. Location (mean, median, mode, geometric mean, etc.)
2. Spread (end points, interquantile range, standard deviation)
3. Skew (clustering toward one end of its range)

Inferential statistics, on the other hand, provide a possible explanation for some described phenomenon that can be applied to the subject property. The explanation is based on probability, i.e., a pattern of chance. In the example above, once the sale price appreciation was *described* in the first step, the second step connected it to the subject property valuation through an *inference*.

Appraisers usually find the most difficulty in the second step. Applying a described event to the subject property implies risk, in that the appraiser's

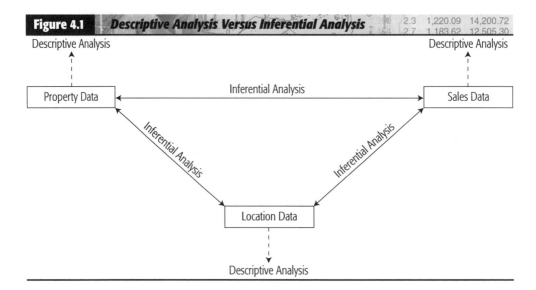

Figure 4.1   *Descriptive Analysis Versus Inferential Analysis*

Descriptive Analysis ↑ Property Data

Inferential Analysis → Sales Data ↑ Descriptive Analysis

Inferential Analysis

Inferential Analysis

Location Data

Descriptive Analysis

judgment and analytical skill are on the line (and in writing). Is that not, however, the prime focus of the appraisal report? Is not the entire valuation process an act of *inferring* value on a given property based on the description of related phenomena? And is it not better to use scientific probability rather than subjective opinion?

Descriptive Statistics

The first descriptive statistics that many students of the subject often encounter are the measures of central tendency: the mean, median, and mode (among others), collectively known as the *average*. In many cases, the *mean* implies the term *average*. However, it is usually better to avoid the term *average* and to be specific as to the meaning intended. Many inferential statistical tools, such as regression analysis, use the mean in their calculation process. The mean average is calculated by listing every value of a variable (such as sale price) and dividing the sum of these values by the number of observations. If the sale file contains 10 sales, then the mean average would be calculated by adding up the 10 sale prices and dividing that total by 10. Obviously, if the sale file contains one transaction that is significantly larger or smaller than the other sales, then the mean average can be affected significantly. If the sale file contains 100 sales, the effect of this same *outlier* would be less.

Using the *median* average to verify the *mean* average is often a good method of checking for unwanted effects of extreme outlier cases. The median average is simply the middle value (i.e., middle-ranked), or the one that occurs at the 50th percentile. If the median and mean averages are similar, then the appraiser can assume that the mean is not affected significantly by any outliers. It does not signify, of course, that outlier cases are not present in the sale file. If an outlier case "pulls" the mean average away from the middle value, then the median and mean averages will not be close to one another. On the other hand, if there are outlier

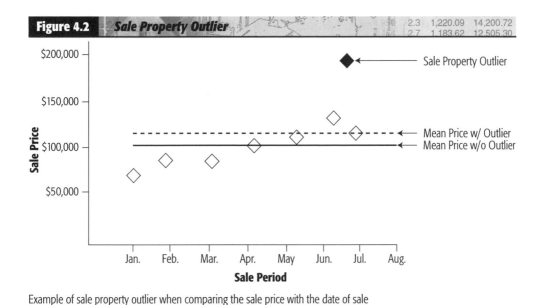

Figure 4.2   *Sale Property Outlier*

Example of sale property outlier when comparing the sale price with the date of sale

cases at both ends of the sale distribution (i.e., sale prices significantly above *and* below the mean average), then the analyst might still want to restrict the analysis to sales that are within a certain distance (or range) from the median value.

The *mode* is the value that occurs most frequently in an array of data. Comparing the mode with the other two measures of central tendency can also support the mean value as an accurate representation of the true average and can help describe how the data are distributed across all values.

When the mode, median, and mean all agree, the appraiser can feel more confident that the distribution of the data (i.e., its spread) is "normal."[1] An examination of the *distribution* of the data, however, is still required.[2]

Graphical Representations of Data

Often the distribution of data can be graphically represented by a *bell-shaped curve,* where most of the values occur in the center (where the mean, median, and modal averages would lie in this case). Another type of data distribution is the *uniform distribution,* where the data are spread out evenly.

The shape of normal (bell-shaped) curves can differ. When examining either a single data set or multiple groups, an analyst should note whether the curve is flat or steep, whether the bell shape is centered over the mean and median values, or whether it is skewed to the right or left. (Note that skewed data will have a similar affect on the mean/median relationship as an outlier.)

---

1. The use of the word here is colloquial rather than statistically precise.
2. Distribution relates to interval-level data, where the differences between numbers is a numerical reality. In nominal or ordinal data, the concept of data distribution is limited. One may speak of how many categories (nominal) or the number of rankings (ordinal) data may possess, but these are general descriptive terms that do not really describe what is going on between data categories. For the purposes of this discussion, sale price distributions will be examined, which are continuous data.

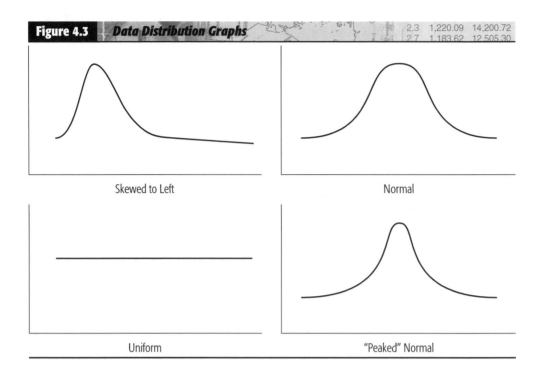

Skewed to Left   Normal

Uniform   "Peaked" Normal

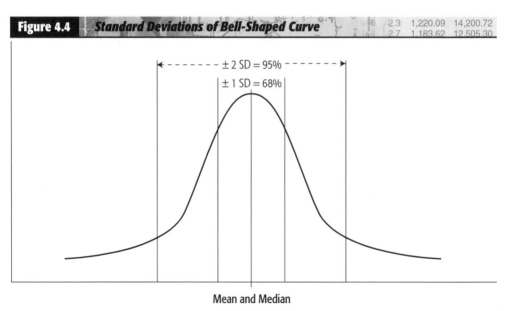

Mean and Median

When data are distributed about the mean/median, the standard deviation can be used to determine the dispersion of data. The area between ± 1 standard deviation would account for 68% of values for a normal distribution, also known as a Gaussian distribution. The area between ± 2 standard deviations would account for 95% of values.

One important measure used in describing data is the *standard deviation*. In mathematical terms, the standard deviation is the square root of the variance, which is defined as the squared differences between individual values of a variable and the mean value. The value of the standard deviation variable can be compared among different variables, even if the variables differ in terms of magnitude or units of measure. In other words, to describe the distribution of both sale price and living area of a sales sample, the distribution of both variables can be compared using the standard deviation. If the sale price standard deviation is 2.3 while the standard deviation of the living area is 5.2, then the data are dispersed more widely for the living area values because 5.2 is greater than 2.3. Notice that nowhere is the sale price or square feet of living area referenced, as it would be if mean or median values were being compared. This makes it possible to compare data distributions of different elements, like sizes and prices.

Tables

There are other descriptive statistical tools available to the user. The *frequency distribution* and *crosstab table* (also known as the *contingency table*) are easy and elegant ways to communicate what a set of data "looks like." The frequency distribution illustrates how many times a value occurs for a particular variable. For example, if an appraiser has 10 homes to analyze, it would be helpful to see the distribution of the gross living areas of these homes. It may also be helpful to see what types of home styles are represented in this 10-home sample. With frequency analysis one can determine if the homes are similar in size and style between one another and with the subject property.

Table 4.1	Frequency Distributions					
GLA	GLA Number	Percent	Style	Home Style Number	Percent
1,200	0	0%	Ranch	4	40%
1,300	2	20%	Bi-level	0	0%
1,400	0	0%	Split-level	2	20%
1,500	1	10%	Two-story	4	40%
1,600	3	30%			
1,700	2	20%			
1,800	0	0%			
1,900	1	10%			
2,000	1	10%			

What if both the size and the style of the home are important considerations? For example, if the subject home is a large ranch home but the 10 comparable sale properties contain only much smaller ranch homes, then using a crosstab table could alert the appraiser that further property characteristic adjustments could be warranted, that two variables are correlated, or that another sample of more comparable properties needs to be collected.

Table 4.2	Example of Crosstab (Contingency) Table			
	House Style			
GLA	**Ranch**	**2-Story**	**Split-Level**	**Total**
1,200	0	0	0	0
1,300	2	0	0	2
1,400	0	0	0	0
1,500	1	0	0	1
1,600	0	0	3	3
1,700	0	1	1	2
1,800	0	0	0	0
1,900	1	0	0	1
2,000	0	1	0	1
Total	4	2	4	10

A frequency or crosstab table can also readily display a market trend variable. The same questions regarding comparability can be answered—e.g., in the comparable sample of 10 homes, the appraiser may want to know *when* these 10 sales occurred during the sale period. In areas of sale price appreciation, it may be important to know that the large ranch home is better represented by earlier sales, when that type of home was selling. A frequency table can easily tell the appraiser if the sale dates are evenly distributed across the sale period (i.e., in a uniform distribution).

Table 4.3	Crosstab Table		
	Ranch Homes–Bedrooms		
Sale Period Month	**2**	**3**	**4**
1	1	2	3
2	0	2	3
3	0	1	4
4	0	0	0
5	1	2	0
6	0	1	0
7	0	2	0
8	0	1	0
9	0	0	0
10	1	0	0
11	0	2	0
12	0	2	0
Total	3	15	10

What if the appraiser wants to compare three or four property characteristics at once? Most statistical programs allow for the use of three- and four-level crosstabs, comparing variables such as size and style and sale date at the same time. However, the use of more than two levels becomes clumsy and only makes sense with larger data sets.

Gross Living Area	Style Ranch	Split-Level
Year = 1997		
1,000	3	1
1,100	1	0
1,200	1	2
Year = 1998		
1,000	2	0
1,100	1	0
1,200	1	0

The crosstab tables above indicate an important limitation of this sales sample, namely, that *all* of the split-level sales occurred in 1997. Any sales trend created by these sales assumes that the ranch home appreciation (if any) can also apply to split-level homes. Does that assumption make sense in an appraisal? The answer is often a qualified yes, particularly when there is no other reasonable alternative method to develop a sales trend. Obviously if this sales sample area is adjacent to another area with split-level home sales in 1998, it may be prudent to combine the two areas and perform a sales trend analysis using only split-level homes. In any case, the limitations of the sales sample should be disclosed to the reader of the report.

Other Descriptive Techniques

Another commonly used descriptive tool is the *boxplot*. Boxplots are excellent graphical tools for comparing data. The mechanics, illustrated in Figure 4.5, are relatively straightforward. The purposes of this type of graphic diagram are to allow the appraiser to quickly verify whether distributions are skewed and whether they are similar across one, two, or more groups. Figure 4.6 shows how boxplots can be used to easily describe the distribution of data and compare data between two or more groups.

Knowing how data are distributed can help an appraiser determine the way the data might behave, which is the subject of the next section on inferential statistical tools.

Figure 4.5 | *Using Boxplot to Describe a Skewed Distribution*

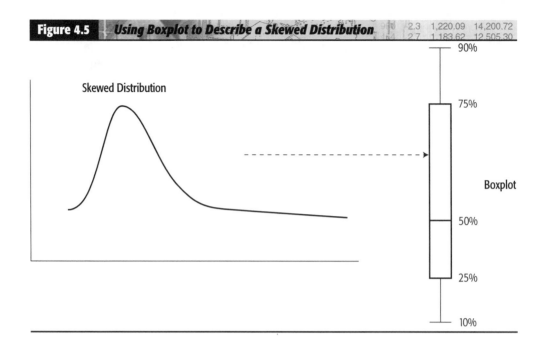

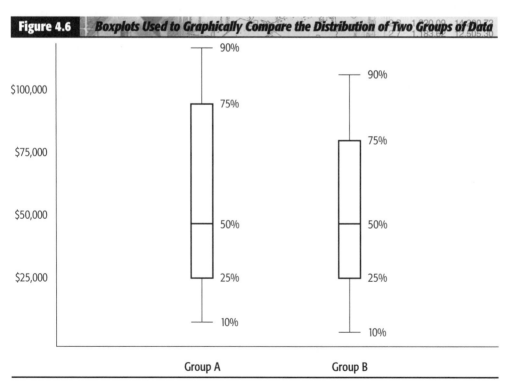

Inferential Statistics

Inferential statistical tools differ from descriptive tools in that the former help the user not only describe the difference between data but also explain the possible association between a set of independent and dependent variables.

The Basics

Independent variables are those that are a given in the analysis—i.e., for which data are available. In the cause and effect language of Chapter 5, the independent variables "cause" the dependent variables to behave in a particular way. Examples of independent variables are property characteristics such as improved area, lot or land area, and the year of construction. In most cases, the dependent variable of interest is the sale price of a property because it most closely approximates a property's value. Although a property's sale price can be thought of as a given when it actually sells, the appraiser is often faced with a property that hasn't yet sold or was sold too long ago for that previous sale price to be relevant. Even if the appraiser is asked to validate a current sale transaction on the subject property, the appraiser must then set aside that sale price and act as if it did not exist. In these cases, the appraiser must look at the set of independent variables to construct a valuation model.

As stated previously, a model can value the entire property or provide an important element in the valuation process. In the case of modeling the entire valuation of the subject property, the dependent variable is the sale price. Independent variables are the factors that affect sale price: the *where* (location), *when* (effective appraisal date), and *what* (property characteristics) of the transaction.

In the case of modeling an important element of the valuation process, such as a market trend adjustment, the dependent variable remains the sale price. Step one would be a model that values the property with all relevant independent variables in the model, including the sales trend factor. The next step would be to extract the sales trend and adjust the sale price of each comparable property by that factor.

Why go through the two-step process if the valuation model contains all independent variables? Indeed, such a model would entail all valuation adjustments, and the appraiser could simply apply these adjustment factors to the subject property directly to arrive at an estimate of value. The reason for the two-step process, and for not using the entire valuation model, has to do with several conditions:

1. The reader of the appraisal may not adequately understand the modeling process and would prefer a manual adjustment "grid" system to explain and derive the valuation of the property.
2. The appraiser may not have all of the relevant data to derive a complete valuation conclusion.

3. Some of the data may be nominal or ordinal and therefore not lend itself to regression-based modeling (at least not in a straightforward manner).

4. The derivation of an adjustment factor may involve variables not directly related to the value of the subject property. For example, if the appraiser is investigating the impact of highway location on a set of data, some of the independent variables used to estimate the effect of highway frontage would not be used in the valuation of the subject property itself.

Inferential Tools

Some inferential tools simply describe the strength of the relationship between the independent variable and the dependent variable. Here strength is measured as the amount of change in the independent variable and the resulting change in the dependent variable. Any unexplained variation in the dependent variable is treated as an unknown or error term.

More powerful inferential statistical tools model, or explain in mathematical terms, the association between independent and dependent variables in a systematic form. For example, regression analysis attempts to build a linear relationship between two sets of variables (generally the dependent variable set has one variable and the independent set has one or more variables). The idea behind regression analysis is that if you change an independent variable by one unit amount, the regression model then changes the dependent variable by a specified amount. Regression analysis can also tell the user the amount of variation the model actually explains.

As an example, inferential tools can be used to describe a set relationship, such as the association between the size of homes and the sale price in a given neighborhood. Here the analysis involves analyzing the data in the file, with the purpose of explaining the relationship between the independent variables and the dependent variable (this process is known as *closed set analysis*). Such an analysis could be used to help estimate the size of adjustments to be used in manual valuation because it involves only the data in the inferential analysis; in other words, all cases under study have both a dependent (sale price) and independent (home size) variable set.

Another useful application involves predicting the value of the dependent (overall value) variable based on the value of the independent (adjustment) variables, known as *open set analysis*. The term *open set* is used because the results of the closed set analysis are then applied to cases where there is no known value for the dependent variable. For example, an analysis of the relationship between the sale price and the size and the number bathrooms of single-family homes in a given area can be readily modeled by regression analysis. This can be limited to a simple study of the effects of housing characteristics on market value (closed set analysis), or the appraiser can use this same information to predict the value of unsold homes in the same area (open set analysis). This second application can be used independently or to be reconciled with traditional sales comparison data grid analysis. As previously illustrated, a two-variable or multiple-variable regression model can help develop the adjustment amounts used in a sales adjustment grid.

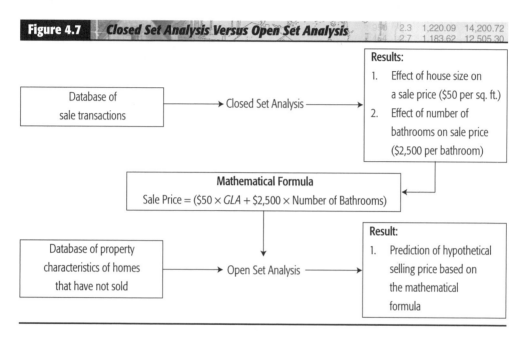

Figure 4.7   Closed Set Analysis Versus Open Set Analysis

Database of sale transactions → Closed Set Analysis →

Results:
1. Effect of house size on a sale price ($50 per sq. ft.)
2. Effect of number of bathrooms on sale price ($2,500 per bathroom)

Mathematical Formula
Sale Price = ($50 × GLA + $2,500 × Number of Bathrooms)

Database of property characteristics of homes that have not sold → Open Set Analysis →

Result:
1. Prediction of hypothetical selling price based on the mathematical formula

Although at first these two applications appear one-and-the-same, the risk varies greatly. To be successful, both closed set and open set analyses need the independent variable set to be comprehensive enough to adequately explain the relationship between the independent and dependent variable sets. Open set analysis *also* requires that the sale sample adequately represent the population of all homes in the area of study. For example, if the regression sales sample includes only ranch-style homes, it may not be a good model for two-story homes in the same area.

Concerns with Inferential Statistics

One issue that needs to be considered is this: Does the sales sample represent the submarket to which the subject belongs (or is the market area properly defined)? Asked another way, are the sales representative of the market the appraiser wishes to analyze? Congruency of independent variables (e.g., year of construction, housing style, lot sizes, garage size) is important because the sample of sale properties will be used to estimate the value of the subject property. If the subject property lacks many of these characteristics or possesses characteristics not included in the sales data, then the appraiser needs to determine whether the subject property is adequately represented by the sales file—i.e., has the competitive market segment been identified?

Real estate knowledge needs to be applied, as with all valuation issues. For example, if a split-level style home in a given neighborhood is being valued and the sale properties under examination are a mixture of split-level, bi-level, and ranch homes, then the the sales sample must include enough split-level homes for a comparison to be meaningful. Generally, a good rule of thumb is that at least six "hits" need to occur for a particular characteristic (in this case, house style = split-level) to be adequately represented. Obviously, if the appraiser is valuing a split-level home and all of the sale properties are ranch homes, there is a problem. Note, however, that this same problem exists even with the traditional sales comparison approach. Data analysis methods can alleviate this type of problem somewhat, but that type of relief is not readily used under traditional methodology.

Another question regarding sampling pertains to sample size: How many sales are "enough" to adequately perform an inferential statistical analysis of the data? The criteria for real estate valuation do not necessarily match those traditionally used in general statistics. Most statistical rules of thumb require 25 to 30 cases (in the example here, sold properties) for a valid sample; however, in valuation analysis the sample is already restricted to the submarket chosen by the analyst. An appraiser must consider several factors:

1. What is the size of the relevant submarket? Is it a 20-unit condominium project or a 220-unit single-family subdivision with only four basic floor plans? Is it a *typical* 22,000-sq.-ft. office building in a market of 4 million leasable square feet? Or is it one of only three high-rises in town?

2. How much general variability exists within the market? Condominium projects can be very similar (i.e., homogeneous); commercial properties, on the other hand, may appear to be so different that no systematic comparison can be made without examining other economic variables. Single-family developments and subdivisions can be between these two extremes, with varying degrees of homogeneity within subgroups.

The descriptive statistical tools described earlier in this handbook may be some of the most effective tools available to understand, analyze, and describe these differences.

Chapter 5

Making a Case for Causation: A Seven-Step Process

2.8	1,256.32	11,200.36
2.6	1,450.35	12,315.09
1.9	1,097.06	14,365.25
3.0	1,250.77	11,256.89
2.5	332.18	10,325.02
		9,385.00
2.3	1,220.09	14,200.72

If it is virtually impossible to prove causation using mathematics, how can an appraiser make a statement in a report that an independent variable has a certain specific influence on the dependent variable? Simply relating two sets of phenomena does not by itself prove that one causes the other. Yet, this leap of analytical faith is what drives the entire process of inferential analysis.

The following seven conditions can help an appraiser decide when to infer causation and when to avoid it. These conditions are necessary, but not sufficient individually, to prove causation, and they should be presented within the framework of the appraisal analysis. Care should be exercised, though, not to overstate certain assumed economic relationships, even when they are supported by the following conditions.

1. Analysis and Bias

The statistical analysis employed to support a causal relationship needs to be as free of bias as possible. For example, suppose the appraiser makes a statement in a report that rising personal income "causes" an increase in the demand for greater retail space in a given area. The appraiser supports this analytical conclusion in the appraisal report with data supplied by the local chamber of commerce.[1] The appraiser needs to be careful that the data themselves are not biased and do not paint an artificially positive economic portrait of the market area. Such a source of data may be supplemented with supporting data from other sources (such as a local university study on retail demand) or even by primary

---

1.   There is also an assumption that greater income creates greater retail space demand, but this assumption is not true in every case. Some "economy-oriented" spaces and locations may be supplanted by luxury or prestige products and locations.

research by the appraiser. The appraiser should always question the source of data and analysis, especially when relying on such secondhand support in their own appraisals.[2]

Bias can also occur within the data collection. One form of this is sampling error, a flaw in the measurement process that is a type of systematic error. An example of sampling error would be a sales data file that purports to represent all single-family homes in an area when in reality it represents only those homes that actually sold. The appraiser must verify if these sales are, in fact, representative. Another example would be a sales sample that represents all homes in a neighborhood where there are two distinctive homebuilders with significant differences in building quality; the higher-quality homes may sell at a greater rate and therefore be overrepresented in the sales sample. The appraiser, in this case, would have to identify the homebuilder in the analysis and treat it as a separate variable to prevent sampling bias from undermining the conclusion of the analysis. The other method of dealing with this problem would be for the appraiser to state that the valuation model pertains only to the higher-quality homes—i.e., to define the relevant submarket, rather than grouping the two submarkets together in the analysis.

The second major source of bias arises from certain types of measurement error. For example, if an appraiser purchases a single-family home sales file from the local assessor's office, that data may contain errors due to measurement mistakes. This can arise from poor building measurements, inconsistent definitions of building characteristics, and other instances where the data reported differ from reality (as covered in Chapter 3). This is a common problem in some MLS data files also.

2. Strength of Association

In many practical cases where the underlying economic theory is sound, a strong measurement of association may support the assertion of causality. If your support is a demonstration of a general relationship, such as the statement "because income is expected to increase over the next five years, an assumption can be made that retail demand will also increase during that same time," the causal link can be difficult to defend, and such a statement can even create doubt in the reader's mind. Assuming that the reader shares the same beliefs (or biases) as the appraiser can be deadly and can lead to problems down the road with lender reviewers and review appraisers.

A more defensible assertion would be an actual measurable statement, such as, "a 5% increase in aggregate income results in a 3% increase in aggregate demand for housing." This causal link assertion would then be supported by some stated mathematical relationship, such as in a regression model.

---

2.   The appraiser needs to understand the differences between Level 1, 2, 3, and 4 studies when relying on these for market analyses in their appraisals. The reader is referred to courses offered by the Appraisal Institute that specifically address the differences (and limitations) of these different levels of market studies.

3. Consistency/Analogy

Can the causal association be proven in differing locales and from differing sources? If the appraiser can cite several sources from different locations, it can help support the case for causation, if it is reasonable to assume the similarity of these markets. Another method to demonstrate consistency would be to use historical data, where the outcome is already known. If precursor conditions in the subject property's market were also present in another market where the outcome is known, then the appraiser's assertion that this same outcome may occur in the subject property's market becomes more reasonable. This approach is similar to one used in the scientific method, where experiments repeatedly yield results that indicate that A causes B.

4. Correct Temporal Relationship

The data and analysis that support causation must have the correct time relationship. For example, if an increase in personal income supposedly causes an increase in retail demand, then the income increase should precede the increase in demand. In other words, if A causes B, then A must occur before B.[3]

5. Dose-Response (Function Relationship)

In some causal relationships, more of X causes more of Y—i.e., the amount of the stimulus has a measurable effect on the amount of the product. In the example of retail demand, a larger increase in personal income can cause a larger increase in retail demand.

Note that some relationships are not linear, meaning an increase in X may cause an increase in Y only after a certain threshold is achieved. For example, an increase in personal income may not affect the demand for luxury homes until a certain income level is reached. Other relationships are the inverse. For example, it is usually the case that a greater traffic count improves commercial property value. In the case of single-family residential, this is normally an inverse relationship. For some situations, it is difficult to generalize except by the analysis of very specific submarkets—e.g., apartments near high-traffic streets may bring less rent due to the noise, smell, and dust factors. In other submarkets, a high-traffic location may cut advertising costs, keep vacancy rates low, or even bring a small rent premium because of the locational identity. Worse yet, these factors can act differently in different economic climates—e.g., in renter's markets and landlord's markets.

The most difficult type of variable to quantify is one that is negatively collinear with another variable but the two always appear together. For example, proximity to high-tension power lines is a detriment to home sites, whether for

---

3.   At least one statistical method is available. The technique assumes that a causal variable will precede the other in time. Two regressions are run—one unrestricted, the other restricted (i.e., a variable is left out). A difference in the two results may indicate causation by the phenomenon occurring earlier.

real or imagined reasons. At the same time, such sites are always adjacent to the open space under the power line, which on its own would be considered an amenity.

6. Plausibility

The stated causal relationship should make appraisal and economic sense. Even if statistical analysis seems to support the statement "X causes Y," if X represents a *decrease* in personal income and Y represents an *increase* in retail demand, the entire construct is in question. The underlying economic or human behavior must "explain" the relationship. This is not an attempt to categorically refute all but obvious causal relationships, but causation is questionable when the stated relationship *ultimately* does not make sense in an appraisal—i.e., it must correlate with some other analytical reason, whether economic theory, personal verification, or survey.

As an example, residential lots in a subdivision were appraised for their retail value (the value of the lots, after approvals and infrastructure were in place, but before homes were constructed). A regression analysis resulted in a negative valuation for walk-out lots (lots with sufficient slope to allow a portion of the basement of the home to be at grade, usually in the rear of the home). Generally, walk-out lots had always been priced at a premium because they tended to make the total living area of the home greater. Upon further examination, however, the analysts realized that the regression model, which included variables accounting for views and lake frontage, was actually measuring the valuation effect of a walk-out lot *after* accounting for these other two items. The following summarizes the coefficient values for walk-out, lake frontage, and view:

Walk-out	– $5,000
Views	$8,000
Lake Frontage	+ $9,000
Net Effect	$12,000

The net valuation of these three factors was $12,000 for a lot with all three characteristics. Obviously, lots without lake frontage and view amenities were not as valuable, and the argument was proffered that such lots were in fact more expensive (because of engineering and lot grading costs) to develop than level lots. The argument that the more expensive lots added value to homes built on them because of the greater value of a walk-out basement could still be made, but the analysts concluded that since the homes that were to be built on those lots were estate-class homes with above-grade living area of over 4,000 square feet, the added value of a walk-out basement was more than offset by the added cost of construction for sloped lots for walk-outs. In this case the statistical analysis lent support to appraisal theory regarding value; it neither overwhelmed that theory nor did it create confusion. The analysis, in fact, pointed out some important issues regarding correctly valuing subdivision lots in areas with varying topography.

7. Specificity

Generally speaking, this occurs when a single effect causes another. More often, many economic factors are banded together and influence several outcomes. Linking one cause with one effect can often say more about the limited scope of the analysis than make a case for causation. Also, that type of specific relationship can be more difficult to defend. The statistical concept of *multicollinearity* has to be considered. It can include the inverse relationship, the correlated independent variables, and underspecified or overspecified formulas. Commonly the elements used in a valuation model are not exactly what the market is considering in the valuation process, but they may be the only measurable phenomena, so appraisers measure them. As always, the appraiser must be sure to describe the limitations in their analyses to the user of the appraisal. Specificity implies low correlation—except the two specific variables, which show a high correlation.

Summary

This chapter on causation is a brief primer on a concept that is often taken for granted by analysts. Causation per se cannot be proven but can be inferred using the seven conditions as supportive evidence.

Any one of these conditions becomes evidence that a causal link *may* exist. Typically, satisfying several of these conditions makes a contention stronger. Satisfying all seven, while a noble goal, is not usually feasible. If the causal link is critical in some way to the appraisal conclusion, however, citing the satisfaction of as many of these conditions as possible is prudent.

Analysts should always question their assumptions regarding causation and clearly state their reasoning. Appraisal knowledge and experience are far more valuable in this situation than any theoretical statistical knowledge. Ultimately the case for causation in an appraisal report is based on the weight of evidence and is not absolute. Statistical tools, combined with appraisal knowledge and experience along with an understanding of the underlying mathematical relationships, make up the key to "correctness." Economic theory (i.e., appraisal theory) often gives a clear concept of causation when mathematics cannot.

	2.8	1,256.32	11,200.36
	2.6	1,450.3	2,315.09
	1.	7	5.25
	3.0	1,250.77	11,256.89
	2.5	1,332.18	10,325.02
	2.6	1,115.60	9,385.00
	2.3	1,220.09	14,200.72

Chapter 6 *Statistical Modeling in the Valuation Process*

The next three chapters put the analytical tools described in the previous chapters to work, providing a statistical framework to help appraisers develop their own statistical analyses or use the output provided by outside sources correctly. This will help appraisers navigate through the myriad of statistical tools and methods available. Mercifully, much of the methodology is familiar territory, albeit with different names. The goal of these chapters is to place that existing knowledge into a systematic framework, ultimately developing a useful method to evaluate, build, and use statistical valuation models in the econometric context.

The focus of Chapters 6, 7, and 8 will be on individual statistical applications that fee appraisers can use in their everyday work environment, starting with automated valuation models (AVMs) in this chapter and moving on to basic regression analysis in the following chapters. It is possible to model entire neighborhoods or even multiple neighborhoods, but most applications will be for the purpose of dealing with an individual property. In essence, mass appraisal is simply an individual appraisal adjusted many times. The principles employed at either level are the same.

Automated Valuation Models and the Appraisal Model

In most automated valuation models (AVMs) and mass appraisal models used by assessors, the appraisal process itself is often programmed into a computer. The AVM seeks out data based on a geographical or neighborhood demarcation and proceeds to "find" appropriate comparable properties. In the case of assessor's models, often 20 or more independent variables are compared against the selling prices of homes in the area. Regression or some other inferential method is then used to derive values as they pertain to the subject property. The process usually involves *all* properties in the given area because the assessor's job is to value all properties for the purposes of fairly distributing the property tax burden across all properties based on legislated rules (i.e., property tax laws).

Some AVMs, on the other hand, value properties one at a time, much like a fee appraiser. The process can be *prospective,* where the valuation algorithm is data-driven and does not start until the user identifies the subject, or it can be *retrospective,* where it is based on predetermined valuation equations (much as with assessor's models). Both have advantages and disadvantages.

The prospective method can be cumbersome to use and may be fairly blind in that the vendor can't check for problems until the value is actually run by the user and problems turn up. An advantage, however, is that the algorithm is dynamic and can be much more current than the retrospective method. The comparable information used can also be dynamically chosen by an algorithm.

The retrospective process has an advantage in that the model's output can be verified up to a certain point. For example, if a modeling area has one home that is significantly older than all of the other homes, the valuation conclusion may be significantly out of the range of the other homes. The retrospective method can determine this event before it is released to the public, whereas the prospective method cannot.

Figure 6.1	Prospective Versus Retrospective AVMs		
Prospective		**Retrospective**	
Step 1.	Sales data updated on regular basis (i.e., monthly, quarterly, weekly). Basic valuation algorithm (equation) created.	Step 1.	Sales data collected; valuation equations are run; output (estimated values) are created for *every* property in study area.
Step 2.	User inputs property address.	Step 2.	Results are checked and compared.
Step 3.	Data and valuation algorithm create value for single property.	Step 3.	User requests value; value is already in data file and is simply extracted.

In either case, the appraiser needs to know the design of whatever AVM is being used or evaluated. The use of an AVM can save effort in many areas but requires that other things be considered and disclosed. The following should be explained in detail in the appraisal report whenever AVM output is used (or when an appraiser-developed model is used):

- Number of sales
- Sales not used and reasons for exclusions
- Sampling veracity (i.e., does the sample represent the whole population or the market?)
- The method used to derive value (regression, artificial intelligence, expert system, etc.)

- Independent variables tested, used, or not used in model
- Area analyzed
- Statistics that measure model accuracy
- Outcome measures (independent/dependent values)
- Clear rationale of the model
- Any other information that may affect the reliability of the valuation process (e.g., source of sales data, source of property data, description of editing process)

These items must be known before the appraiser can effectively evaluate the output from the AVM (or any valuation model). This includes models designed by the appraiser.

Most AVMs are good at estimating the value of properties with homogeneous property characteristics and location factors. With appraiser-based market estimate modeling, however, the valuation process that an appraiser uses can be more refined and meaningful because it may better reflect the concerns that the actual real estate market mechanism presents in a defined neighborhood. In other words, the appraiser need only be concerned with the actual variables that go into the valuation of the property. While many variables can be initially scrutinized by the appraiser, the resulting model used will usually have only a small set of variables used to predict value. The goal of the appraiser should be to develop the simplest, most straightforward model possible (the concept known as *parsimony*). The appraiser should be more concerned with effectively modeling the sales market than attempting to construct the most complex model possible.

Primary Variables

When people purchase their homes, there are usually several important factors that influence all sales in the same neighborhood. Location is the most critical of these. Next, the size of the home, expressed as square feet of total living area, number of bedrooms and bathrooms, or a combination of these. Other variables, such as year of construction, house style, subdivision, number of car spaces, lot size, and basement finished square footage can also play a significant role. All of these can be considered primary variables in the modeling process; the set of primary variables, however, can vary from market to market.

Most buyers have an upper-limit price constraint, coupled with certain minimal levels of amenity preference. For example, minimal levels may include location, bedrooms, baths, and overall size. Strong preferences for certain characteristics (say quality, view, new kitchen, or yard size) may also act like these

> *When people purchase their homes, what are the common factors that influence all sales in the same neighborhood?*

primary characteristics. These tend to define the market for a particular buyer or class of buyers—i.e., certain people in the market for homes with a specific set of characteristics. These groups of consumers create a strong market linkage between primary property variables and sales prices. Statistically these variables are highly significant because they are important to the market. Some of these variables, such as living area, are easy to measure and are relatively precise. Others are more difficult to measure, such as the market value of an amenity such as views or water frontage.

Secondary Variables

Variables such as fireplaces, garage type, pool, and air conditioning may also be significant and be included in the model. While these secondary variables have some market impact, they are less often significant in the regression model. Although these variables can influence decisions within a market segment (class), they do not usually define the market segment. Nevertheless, they can be important if there is little difference (i.e., variation) in certain primary variables. For example, if a neighborhood has homes that were all built within a two-year period and all possess between 1,400 and 1,600 square feet of living area, then two primary variables, age and gross living area, may be excluded from the model—because there is little variation within the market, not because the market would not respond to them. Other factors such as fireplaces, size of garage, or floor plan may play a more important role in that particular market.

Other Variables

Finally, there is a third set of variables that will be used even less often yet may motivate certain buyers to varying degrees. Such variables may influence only occasional buyers or have small value relative to the overall decision. Examples of these are location of the laundry area, guest closet, fencing, flooring, or patio. Some AVMs—those that use a combination of regression and heuristics (human or feedback refinement of adjustment amounts)—will use other support for these adjustments, as would an appraiser using traditional methodology. Variables of this third level tend to be subjective or calculated by another method: construction quality, physical condition, and functional utility, for example. They may be important in certain applications or submarkets, but caution must be exercised because these independent variables are difficult to quantify or are subjective. (However, note that as data fields input continues to improve, these elements of comparison will become more measurable and less subjective.)

> *In the market transaction process, what common variables actually influence market preference for typical purchasers?*

Combinations

Out of the many possible variables, the typical regression model may arrive at five or six variables that are actually used in the model. The appraiser addresses what common variables actually influence market value for typical purchasers. In a neighborhood where all homes have detached, two-car garages, one would expect that garage type and garage spaces (or size) would probably not come into the valuation equation.

Modeling and Appraisal

Is it reasonable to build a model with more than 30 variables, particularly when the buyers respond mostly to five or six primary factors?

Automated valuation models, in most cases, properly refer to preprogrammed appraising models. The difference between this and professional market value estimation is profound.

The modeling process should always be under the constraints and control of the appraisal process, not the other way around. This important distinction also applies to other automation schemes, such as artificial intelligence and iteration-based models (where valuation is part of a step-by-step automated process). Most of these valuation schemes are often thought of as attempts to replicate the appraisal process, and hence the appraiser, with a computer. Instead, by placing this analytical paradigm *into* the appraisal process and not over it, the statistical analysis and modeling process can correctly become a tool and a marketable product for appraisers. For users, the appraisal product is more precise, more robust, and more comprehensive.

For years governmental assessment analysts (i.e., mass appraisers) have grappled with large, unwieldy statistical models to value residential properties within their jurisdictions. Some assessment-based models contain more than 30 variables to predict the market value of residential properties. These variables can include add-on items such as hot tubs, front and rear porches, finished attics, wood decks, patios, and even built-in barbecues. Common sense forces appraisers, when presented with these composite approaches to valuation, to determine if it is reasonable to build a model with that many variables, particularly when buyers respond mostly to five or six primary factors.

One of the rules of analysis is that any phenomenon under scrutiny that one wishes to predict or explain must be typical, meaning that one would expect that people behave in a pattern that is roughly repeatable and quantifiable. For example, if 100 people purchasing 100 different homes in the same area purchased those homes for unique reasons, it would be impossible to quantify the major factors contributing to real estate value. Fortunately, in most markets people sell and purchase real estate for similar, quantifiable reasons.

Under laboratory conditions, a market value of a property could be derived if a large number of people were allowed to bid on the same property. This bidding process would factor out the conditions of a sale that affect its arm's-length nature, and the value could be displayed as a distribution, with a mean sale price and standard deviation. One could then compare this sale price bid with other similar properties. The problem with this scenario is that it does not reflect the imperfect real world. Home purchasers do not generally show up at an auction to bid on single properties. The real estate purchase mechanism usually results in single offers for single properties. What mass appraisal approaches offer, however, is the ability to *approximate* the multiple-bid process. By valuing properties based on multiple sales in a given area, with general property homogeneity, the value estimate derived using mass appraisal techniques can often be the next best option to the multiple-bid scenario.

Traditional mass appraisal methods have originated with county assessors, who are confined by the goals and the realities of the ad valorem tax process. The county assessor usually builds mass appraisal models with wide nets—that is, models with many variables—partly because the goal of the assessor's valuation process is an equitable distribution of the tax burden across *all* properties. For example, if the assessor consistently undervalues properties in a jurisdiction by 10%, the net impact on the effective tax burden is zero. The property tax load is distributed across properties by the same effective tax rate (i.e., the mill levy would be higher for all properties by the same factor). The problem with models based on the methodologies used by assessors arises when properties are not valued equitably. For example, if one neighborhood is undervalued in comparison to a similar neighborhood in the same jurisdiction, then owners of homes in the former area would pay less property tax than owners of homes in the latter. Assessor models, therefore, focus on equity, rather than on individual market valuation veracity.

On the other hand, appraisal models for an individual property must focus on the variables (elements of comparison) most relevant to that property. Therefore only variables that significantly affect value are included—that is, variables that approximate the market mechanisms determining real estate value in a specific market. Combining human interface in market definition and variable selection (along with property inspection and identification of parameters) with appraisal theory *atop* statistical methods results in perhaps the best market value approximation possible.

Market-based, computer-assisted statistical analysis modeling can offer appraisers a concise modeling approach with a reliable market value estimate in many instances. And by approximating the market transaction, it allows the appraiser to evaluate the model using appraisal theory. Users will possess a product that is more objective, that is reproducible, and that provides a confidence/reliability measure.

Chapter 7

The Concept of Regression

Imagine building a straight road across the United States that touches both the Atlantic Ocean and the Pacific Ocean at each end. The person building this road wishes to place it as close as possible to the 50 largest population centers. What procedures could the builder employ to do that?

The first step would be to identify population centers in the United States—for this example, say, the 50 largest cities in the country. The second step would be to plan the road's location to achieve the shortest distances from every city. Ultimately the sum of the distances from the road to each city should be minimized.

Certain statistical techniques can be used to determine the position of this road by first placing its midpoint in the population center of the United States relative to the 50 largest cities (say, somewhere in rural Illinois or Missouri). The eastern portion of the country will influence the placement of the road more than the western U.S. because more of the large cities are located in that part of the country. Then, that line is moved by pivoting it on its center point. Imagine the roadway moving like a seesaw until the *total* distance from the line to every city is minimized.

This idea is the essence of the least squares method of regression analysis. The line that best fits the scatter plot of U.S. cities is analogous to the type of linear equation that an appraiser would find useful for modeling market behavior. Although no cities are actually on the line, it is the *best* estimate of nearness to a large city.

A Primary Tool

Once the analytical scope of this sort of problem is defined, a mathematical modeling program can be used to create algebraic coefficients based on a unique set of variables. This set may vary between modeling areas, even with areas that

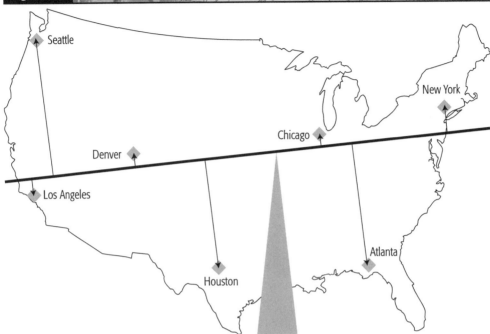

| Figure 7.1 | Example of Building Regression Line Using U.S. Cities | 2.3 | 1,220.09 | 14,200.72 |
| | | 2.7 | 1,183.62 | 12,505.30 |

Pivot point is where 50% of population is located on both sides.

Final version of line would minimize the distance (represented by the arrows) between cities and line.

appear to be similar overall, because the variables used in the model are selected by the available data. When analysts use this type of mathematical model to estimate property value, they will enter all the available data into their model, but the variables actually used by the model will be based on market performance. If fireplaces don't add to value in a particular neighborhood, then their presence in a home will not be included as a variable in the valuation process.

Fortunately, software packages on the market today can make the mechanics of all this fairly easy. (The challenge is in the interpretation and the reporting—processes in which appraisers are trained.) The most common comprehensive modeling processes use multiple regression analysis. Simpler or two-variable processes can be used for other purposes, such as adjustment support and visual analysis.

Linear[1] regression is a powerful tool in inferential analysis and has received a great deal of attention over the past 40 years. Mathematically, the least squares

---

1. It is important to recognize that few economic relationships in this area are truly linear. Non-linearity can be handled in several ways:

   - The assumption of linearity over a small range is often a reasonable approximation of the curve. Appraisers universally use this assumption. The choice of "good" comparables reduces any error due to this assumption.

   - There is some evidence that the motivation of buyers is somewhat linear over a range where their needs are satisfied, with distinct change in the curve slope at the ends of the range.

   - Mathematical transformation. Any curve can be transformed into a linear relationship first—e.g., just like dollars per square foot can be converted to Euros per square meter, curvature can be reduced, increased, or linearized. The remaining linear relationship can then be analyzed through least squares or other measures of strength of relation.

approach (the most common form of regression analysis) is error-prone and discouraging when done by hand, and it is clumsy and time-consuming on an electronic calculator. On the other hand, the repetitious calculations of this process are particularly suited to computerization, and the information can be transferred electronically from a data source with great ease.

Regression analysis has received attention partly as a result of the advent of personal computers and partly because of its inherent elegance as a way to relate and interpret the relationships between two or more variables (such as sale price and gross living area). Another reason for the popularity of regression analysis is because it is a robust process adaptable to any number of scientific and business applications to enhance decision making abilities.

Least Squares Approach

The least squares process uses the square of the distances to the regression line. Squared numbers are used for two reasons:

1. Squaring any number yields a positive number.
2. Squares simplify many other mathematical relationships.

For a residential property, typical variables include living area, basement area, number of bedrooms and bathrooms, and the property's value (i.e., the dependent, or response, variable). In general, regression analysis tests each variable entered into the model and performs two steps simultaneously:

1. It evaluates the relative importance of the variables to value (based on statistical probability theory).
2. It creates a valuation formula that has the smallest "distance" (the least squares) between the estimated sale price and the actual sale price of every property in the sale area (analogous to the example of the distance between the road across the U.S. and the population centers).

This distance, known as *error* or *deviation*, is based on all sales used. Obviously, if one sale differs from all the others by a sizable amount, the error with that particular sale can greatly affect the outcome of the analysis. Conversely, caution must be exercised because the analyst does not want to tailor the data to fit into a preconceived pattern. The key factor is that appraisal theory leads the analysis by defining the market area or market segment. Every sale inside the market segment is included (or specifically deleted for a reason), and everything outside the market area is not included in the analysis.

Applying the Least Squares Method

The example used in this chapter includes 10 single-family sales in the same sub-neighborhood. The variable of interest, the sale price, is the dependent variable. Its value depends on the values of the other variables in the regression analysis.

These independent variables are the verifiable housing characteristics available from a county assessor, multiple listing service, or other data source. Note that the sale prices of these properties are also part of the data set, but in this analysis an assumption can be made that the sale price is influenced by these independent variables in some way (which is why it is the *dependent* variable).

The corollary to regression analysis from traditional appraisal methodology is the table used on the Uniform Residential Appraisal Report (URAR) form. Like an adjustment grid, a regression model, in a slightly different form, relates changes in one or more independent variables to a dependent variable of interest (i.e., the estimated sale price). The general form of the regression equation (for two independent variables) is this:

Dependent Variable = Constant + (Coefficient × Independent Var 1) + (Coefficient × Independent Var 2)

Or, for example:

Estimated Sale Price = Value Constant* + ($50 × Living Area Square Feet) + ($25 × Basement Square Feet)

* This constant should not be interpreted as a site value of properties in the neighborhood.

The adjustment values for square feet of living area and square feet of basement area are developed in the regression analysis. The values are those that result in the equation that produces the smallest squared residuals (i.e., the differences between each value and the average). These values are then multiplied by the values from the subject data source. The estimated sale price is then computed for each of the 10 sale properties. Note two important facets of this regression analysis:

1. The appraiser cannot enter what the owner or lender *thinks* the property is worth. In other words, the process is blind to the expectations of concerned parties.
2. An actual sale price does exist for each comparable.

The calculation compares the estimate of sale price with the actual sale price for each of the sold properties.

This comparison of the expected sale price to the actual sale price generates other statistics such as R^2, one measure of how "good" the model is. Another important statistic is the coefficient of variation (COV), which is essentially the average difference between the actual sale price and the estimated sale price for the 10 sale properties, usually expressed as a percentage. This statistic is often used in assessor's offices to measure the relative accuracy of a mass appraisal.

Once the model is evaluated for accuracy (which will be discussed later in this chapter), the next step is to apply the model's coefficient values (*similar* to adjustment amounts) to the subject property itself. This process is much like the traditional sales comparison table, where the subject property is compared with the sale properties. What is different here is that the regression model provides

the appraiser with the actual values for each significant valuation factor, such as square feet of living
area, lot size, age of improvements, number of
bathrooms, square feet of basement area, etc.

> **What determines an appropriate fit for a model?**

Note that regression coefficients are usually
different (i.e., larger) than what an appraiser typically uses. The adjustments in the sales comparison
approach are analogous to the coefficients in a regression analysis model, but
the two sets of values are not usually equivalent. (Regression coefficients "grab"
part of the adjustment for other variables—e.g., if *room count* is not in a regression, *square feet* will incorporate part of that "missing" variable's coefficient. In
fact, it will grab part of every variable not in the equation with which it is
correlated.)

Output Statistics

When regression analysis is used, various statistics (or indices) are generated by the
model to indicate whether the *fit* of the model is "good" based on some range of
acceptability. What determines an appropriate fit? This depends on the subject of
the analysis, which provides guidance from outside the field of statistics or mathematics. The particular discipline (i.e., economic theory) defines what ranges are
acceptable. For example, soy bean farmers may have much less stringent accuracy
requirements for predicting soy bean futures than commercial aircraft engineers
designing metal fatigue tolerances of new metal alloys, even though both may be
using the same statistical measurement of accuracy. One question worth asking
when determining statistical tolerances is the cost of being wrong. The cost to the
farmer for overestimating demand for soy beans is probably less than the cost of
underestimating the wing tensile strength on a commercial aircraft. An appraiser's
need for precision probably falls somewhere in between these two applications,
influenced by the particular appraisal problem. For example, if only the sales
comparison approach to value a property is used, the fit of the model may need to
be fairly tight, as compared to another appraisal problem where the other approaches to value are also used to verify the estimate of value generated by the
sales comparison approach (why AVMs work well for homogeneous neighborhoods). The fit will depend on the data. If an appraiser is valuing a tract home in a
fairly homogeneous neighborhood, the regression model estimates should be
falling between ±5% of actual values, based on the authors' experience.

The Coefficient of Determination (R^2)

Many output statistics are available from statistical software programs. The R^2
statistic (also known as the *coefficient of determination*) ranges from 0.00 to 1.00,
with 1.00 being the desired value. A high number, say, 0.9427, means that
approximately 94% of the value can be explained by the variables (i.e., the

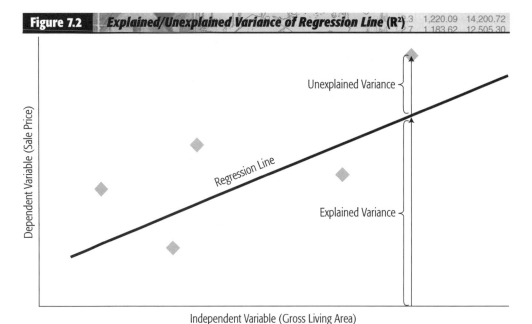

Figure 7.2 — **Explained/Unexplained Variance of Regression Line (R²)**

The R² statistic is the ratio of explained variation to the total variation. The unexplained variation, also known as the *error,* is the difference between the total variation and the explained.

elements of comparison in the sales comparison approach). The R^2 value is sometimes expressed in terms of a percentage, so that an R^2 of 0.25 becomes 25%, an R^2 of 0.9326 becomes 93.26%, etc. It is the ratio of the *explained* sum of squares and the *total* sum of squares, thus the *unexplained* ratio.

That 93% represents the amount of variation explained or determined by the regression model. The general rule of thumb is that any regression model used in real estate valuation with an R^2 greater than 60% explains a lot. A model with an R^2 near 1.0000, or 100%, describes the sale price relationship perfectly. In the 10-sale example, the estimated sale prices would match the actual sale prices exactly. (Every sale would be on the line, perfectly determined, like in most theoretical paired-sales analyses.)

The R^2 statistic describes the general explanatory power of a model, but an analyst must also look at the significance, direction, and strength of the individual coefficients. Furthermore, the R^2 statistic does not provide a useful measure of how accurate the model is for a specific property. Knowing the model's *average error* is usually more useful to those concerned with the predictive power of a regression-based valuation model because the average error statistic describes the expected error on an *individual* basis whereas R^2 measures the *total* fit of the equation. In other words, an R^2 of 75% might be statistically interesting and worth noting in the appraisal report, but a measurement of the average error (expressed as a percent) is a much more useful tool for evaluation.

Coefficient of Variation

The coefficient of variation (COV) measures average error. This statistic is generally useful for models with, say, more than 25 comparable sales. Used for years by county assessors in mass appraisal modeling, COV is a good measure of how well the model can predict the value of homes in the modeling area. The appraiser needs to know the physical characteristics of the subject home and how it relates to the sale properties, much as with the sales comparison approach. Any transaction adjustments (such as financing and sale conditions) to account for differences between the sale property and the arrayed sales would have to be considered before applying the output variables to the subject property.

Coefficient of Dispersion

For regression models using fewer than 25 sales, another "average error" statistic, known as the *coefficient of dispersion* (COD), is the preferred measurement. While COV divides the standard deviation by the mean sale price, COD divides the absolute deviation by the median sale price. The term *deviation* is synonymous with *difference*, in this case the difference between the actual sale price and the estimated sale price of each sale. Both the COV and COD statistics derive a percentage measure of accuracy by dividing the average difference between the estimated and actual sale price by the average sale price; they differ in the way they calculate the average difference:

COV: Standard deviation / Mean sale price

COD: (Absolute average deviation / Median sale price) $\times$ 100

COV is calculated by squaring each deviation (the differences between the actual and estimated sale price), adding these squared deviations together, dividing by the number of sales, and then taking the square root. In other words, the standard deviation of the sale price is divided by the mean sale price. COD, on the other hand, is calculated by taking the absolute value of each deviation, summing these values, and then taking the average. This average absolute deviation is then divided by the median sale price.

Arithmetical Considerations

Why all the squaring and absolute valuing? If you simply add the deviations, you may get a sum of zero because some of the deviations are negative and others are positive. The COD method takes the absolute value (i.e., pretends they are all positive), while the COV method takes a square (i.e., any number multiplied by itself yields a positive product) and then takes a square root to get back to the original unit of measure. The following table illustrates the differences between each method with a small sales sample:

Sale	Estimated Sale Price	Difference from Mean	Squared Difference	Absolute Difference
1	$100,000	– $5,000	$25,000,000	$5,000
2	$105,000	$0	$0	$0
3	$110,000	+ $5,000	$25,000,000	$5,000
4	$100,000	– $5,000	$25,000,000	$5,000
5	$110,000	+ $5,000	$25,000,000	$5,000
Mean/Total	$105,000	$0	$100,000,000	$20,000

Simply adding up the differences in this example yields a sum of zero. The COV difference results in a total squared difference of $100 million; this amount is then divided by four (the number of sales – 1), and then the square root is taken. When the result of those operations is divided by the average sale price, the result is 4.76%. The COD method takes the $20,000 total deviation, calculates the mean ($4,000) and divides this by the median average $105,000, resulting in a ratio of 3.8%.

COV	
1.	$100,000,000 / (5 – 1) = $25,000,000
2.	sqrt($25,000,000) = $5,000 (standard deviation)
3.	$5,000 / $105,000 = 0.0476
4.	0.0476 × 100 = 4.76% (COV)

COD	
1.	$2,000 / 5 = $4,000 (average absolute deviation)
2.	$4,000 / $105,000 = 0.0381
3.	0.0381 × 100 = 3.81% (COD)

Looking at the arrayed data illustrates that the COD may be more meaningful for very small groups of data; the COV works better with larger sale amounts. Because appraisers are often faced with relevant sale samples smaller than 25 sales, the COD is probably the preferred statistic for "manual" analysis while COV works better in computerized analysis and is generally adequate for even a small sample set. Other methods of weighting variance are available.

Both the COD and COV take their respective deviation totals and divide them by either the mean sale price (in the case of the COV) or the median sale price (in the case of the COD). What happens if you divide by the wrong average sale price? Generally, when you calculate the COV or the COD with large sale totals (greater than 25), there is not much difference because the mean and median averages tend to be very close. In small samples, however, the mean and median can differ significantly, so caution is recommended whenever using these statistics when the sale total is less than 30. (One way of remembering is that the COD uses the meDian as its divisor, not the mean.) The COD is generally better for straight analysis, being based on the median, which is less susceptible to the influence of outliers. The COV is better for more sophisticated models, where further mathematical manipulation takes place.

Most computer programs that calculate regression models provide the R^2 statistic as part of their standard output. Getting the COV or COD, on the other hand, may be more problematic. One way to approximate it with standard output is to take the regression standard error, which is always supplied, and divide that number by the average sale price. This method provides a good COV clone. Because it better approximates the COV (and not the COD), caution should be exercised with files of fewer than 30 sales, however.

Another cautionary note concerns any atypical sales. For example, assume a comparable sales analysis uses 10 sales, nine of them ranging between $100,000 and $120,000 with an average error of 6%. The 10th sale, with a sale price of $200,000 and an error of 10%, is added to the model. The COV statistic will be greater than the COD statistic, based on the influence of the $200,000 sale on the mean sale price. On average, the COV will tend to overstate variation and therefore understate the accuracy of the model if it is used in smaller sale samples. Of course, it is probably better to have a statistic that tends to overstate the average error of a model than to understate it, so this approximation method can still be useful when getting the COD statistic proves difficult. In other words, you are probably doing better than the COV is telling you.

What is a Good Model?

What is an acceptable range of accuracy for the COV of a regression-based appraisal model? Less than 7–10% average error is considered acceptable in most cases. A model under 5% is considered very good, but in any case appraisal principles become the guiding protocol.

Even if model accuracy is acceptable, the same principles used in traditional appraisal applications still apply. The subject property needs to be similar enough to the comparable sales for the valuation estimate to be reasonable. For example, assume that the subject property in your analysis is in a deteriorated condition while all of the sale properties in the model are in average condition. The appraiser must adjust the model estimate of value for the subject property by some factor to account for the subject property's deteriorated condition. This may be done through adding a separately derived statistical variable (or by manual adjustment) before or after the regression run. If the subject property doesn't have a characteristic that all comparables have, then the model will not be able to account for that characteristic mathematically as it applies to the

What is an acceptable range of accuracy for the COV of a regression-based appraisal model?

subject (given the lack of variation in that characteristic in the available data). Perhaps the appraiser in this case would need to create a model that analyzes the effect of property condition on sale price, looking at a group of average properties with another group of properties in below-average condition. If done properly, these global adjustment factors can be used with many appraisals, whenever the issue of property condition comes into play. We used to call this "experience."

Adjustment Factors

Whether the modeling process is performed to create a comprehensive valuation model or to assist in deriving individual adjustment amounts for a traditional appraisal does not negate the need to follow the recognized methods of the sales comparison (or other) approach. The issues of property rights conveyed, terms of sale, conditions of sale, expenditures immediately after the sale, and market conditions are all pertinent to the appraisal modeling process. In other words, the sale price may need to be adjusted for these factors using traditional appraisal adjustment methods (such as using cash equivalency adjustments in the case of atypical market financing of a property sale) *before* the regression model is used. Alternatively a two-variable (ANOVA) analysis on just the one dependent variable may provide a well-supported adjustment. Transaction and time adjustments are seldom collinear with any physical or capitalization elements. If this is not done, then the results of the regression model may be wrong—a case of garbage in, garbage out. Adjustment for these factors, as in the case of traditional sales adjustment methods, must be done *prior* to adjustments for location and property characteristics. Market conditions (time) and other non-realty elements may be adjusted via any method available, including as a variable within regression, as a separate grouped-pair adjustment, or other method. Location adjustments with regression-based modeling can be accomplished through the use of dummy variables, which is discussed in Chapter 8.

The elements of comparison that must be considered first are related to the contract or the transaction rather than to the property or the market. This does not mean that there are not market responses to certain contract transaction features. Adjustments to sale prices to account for factors impacting the arm's-length nature of the comparable sales should be estimated and made *prior* to the rest of the modeling process, whenever possible.

Market Conditions (Time)

One of the primary variables that needs scrutiny involves changing market conditions (price trend). Comparable sale prices must be adjusted before physical, location, and economic factors are accounted for. Since regression modeling can analyze physical and location factors in one step, the appraiser can test for any sale price appreciation while at the same time controlling for these other valuation factors.[2]

Other unexpected changes over the sale period can also happen. These are changes that must be accounted for before any analysis is performed to estimate appreciation in sale price. These changes in the definitions of variables can significantly affect the appraisal analysis. If the appraiser cannot adjust for these changes, the analysis may have to be terminated.

If, for example, the appraiser uses county assessor's data in the sales database and the assessor changes the definition of gross living area during the sales period, then an adjustment to the data will have to be made. Even if these differences can be controlled for, caution must be exercised when interpreting them. For example, assume the county data source includes finished basement square footage in gross living area at the beginning of the sale period but ex-cludes that variable beginning with the second half of the period due to a change in definition. Even if an appraiser can distinguish the finished basement area from the living area totals of the first half, the data may still be difficult to compare. Are the finished basement totals reliable enough? Were they collected and verified in the same manner for both periods? It may be that the variable should be excluded from the model entirely. It may also be that the entire database would need to be verified with the county again. Changes in the way real estate boards enforce their data entry rules can also impact valuation.

Another issue with the measurement of market trends is the distribution of comparable sales across the sales period. For example, for defining an adjustment for market conditions, the sales should occur fairly evenly throughout the time period in question, looking more like a uniform distribution. If the sale period covers two years and nine out of ten of the sales occur during the first two months, then the derived appreciation (or depreciation) market trend may be skewed by any random factor or unmeasured influence in the 10th factor. Building a trend based on that form of distribution is not much more reliable than the support provided by a single pair, perhaps the poorest known form of support (pretending to be objective). Remember that the ultimate goal of any temporal analysis is to project the trend into the date of value based on accurate and consistent historical data. This atten-tion to clustering applies to any variable used in the model.

Strategies for Dealing With Market Trend Adjustments

One approach to account for the changes in market levels over a sample period is simply to treat it as any other continuous variable. As a continuous variable,

---

2. Grouped pair support is one way to deal with a price trend. Compare the most recent six months median prices to those over a six-month period one year ago. This is a simple but effective way to support an adjustment when the data are restricted to economically competitive properties but there are at least several data points in each cluster. Comparing periods one year apart controls for seasonal effects. Alternatively it could be argued that seasonal effects are a part of the value as of a specific date and should be included in the analysis. Within a regression, time can be handled as a continuous variable, a discrete variable (e.g., number of months before), or dummy variables (i.e., a 1 or 0 for each period of time to be considered). The dummy variable approach partially resolves the linearity assumption.

Figure 7.3 Effect of Market Trend on Sales Data

Sale 1

Sale 2

Sale 3

Sale 4

Sale 5

Market Trend Adjustment

Sale 6

Beginning
Jan. 1998

End
Dec. 1998

12-Month Sale Period

In effect, the market trend adjustment moves every sale forward to the end of the sale period.

time can be entered into the statistical analysis and controlled for. Measured in days prior to date of value, time can be used by the appraiser to adjust the dependent variable of the subject. Alternatively and for reporting clarity, the appraiser could adjust the sale price of every comparable sale by the appropriate market trend factor and then rerun the appraisal model using the time-adjusted sale price. Of course, in this second run, time would be removed as an independent variable because it is already included "in" the sale price.

For example, assume that 20 sale properties are used to calculate the value of homes in a particular subdivision. Next, assume that these 20 properties sold over a one-year period. If the statistical analysis determines that properties have been appreciating by the rate of 1% per month, then these properties would be adjusted by that amount, depending on the month the property sold. A comparable property that sold during the first month of the sale period would be adjusted upward by 12% (or 1% times 12 months), a property sold six months into the sales period would be adjusted upward by 6%, and so forth. Assumptions necessary for model accuracy would include that the appreciation was constant (no significant seasonal fluctuations) and that other significant differences were accounted for in the first model run, either through restriction to directly comparable properties or through regression. These other differences would include the usual array of physical characteristics, such as living area, style, and age. In effect, a time trend amount that adjusts the sale price takes time completely out of the picture, as if every sale occurred at the end of the time period. Next, these adjusted sale prices would be used and the statistical analysis would be rerun to determine the estimate of value equation with all significant variables except for time.

An alternative method would be to simply leave in time as a variable and create the valuation equation with time in the model among all the other variables. In this instance, the estimate of value is as of the sale date, not at the end of the sale period. The overall effect is generally the same as the previous method, but the appraiser must understand the subtle differences between both approaches.

The following example illustrates how time would be coded in this analysis:

Sale	Sale Date	Sale Amount	Coded Time Value
1	01/99	$100,000	12
2	12/99	$110,000	1
3	06/99	$108,000	6
4	09/99	$107,000	4
5	04/99	$103,000	9

The beginning month of the time period is coded as the last month in the time period, while the last month of the period is coded as the number 1; if it is a two-year span, then sales occurring in the first month would be coded as 24. The reason for this reverse order is that this allows for the time value derived from the model to be positive. Other time periods, such as quarters and semi-annual periods, could also be used instead of months.

Again, if the model determines that time is a significant factor, then the appraiser can adjust the sale price much as adjustments made for time are performed on sale adjustment grids. Or the appraiser can simply run the model with time and the other variables included.

Chapter 8

Building a Regression Model

This chapter will take the reader through a step-by-step process of creating a regression-based appraisal model. This process applies to both a comprehensive model where property valuations are the goal of the appraisal model and to a limited set of variable estimates to be used in a traditional adjustment table (this can also be used to make market-derived adjustments for external obsolescence). The purpose of this section is to define the steps that need to take place to actually create data-centric appraisal models.

A residential appraisal model has been used as an example because these types of models have initially been the most popular applications of regression-based appraisal analysis and provide understandable commonalities for income or amenity properties. The same step-by-step process can be applied to other appraisal problems, though, such as subdivision analysis and most commercial applications, especially when deriving adjustment factors.

The appraiser must resolve questions about data and data sources. The data frame (i.e., market area) must be defined. The data themselves must be analyzed for quality, relevance, and completeness. Any data correction or enhancement must be done before any modeling can begin. The first several steps of building a regression model concern the preparation of the sales file. The following steps deal with the mathematical modeling process itself. These modeling steps will be presented in a generic format that can apply to any of the popular spreadsheet and statistical software packages.[1] Most popular spreadsheets are capable of providing the needed calculations either directly or through simple preparation of a template. Add-on packages are also available for spreadsheets and are more

---

1. In the analyses of the examples here, SPSS statistical software has been used, but most any statistical package or spreadsheet add-on will do.

than adequate for most basic valuation analyses. However, statistical packages are much quicker once they have been set up.

Step 1. Identification of the Modeling Area(s)

First the appraiser must understand how property data are grouped so that the appropriate data groups match the market area for the subject property. The way data are organized can help or harm analysis for certain purposes. MLS data are often grouped by and for real estate agents, rather than for a systematic grouping analysis by appraisers. Many databases of county assessors distinguish between neighborhoods and subdivisions using neighborhood identification numbers, which makes these groupings generally superior to those found in MLS sources. Census tract groupings are quite useful and are becoming readily available. The use of more than one data source is better than using only one, but merging multiple data sources that do not have similar data modeling structures can be difficult. This is not always the case, though; appraisers should first check with both data sources to determine which has the best grouping construct. The relevant market area is, of course, to be determined by appraisal theory, not statistical theory.

Grouped data are usually provided by the county in a comprehensive manner. Often an appraiser can obtain the assessor's subdivision or neighborhood numbers at a nominal charge, and certain Internet-based data sources will download sales based on subdivision numbers. It is critical that the appraiser understands how the neighborhoods are identified. For example, a neighborhood may be known in the community by a single name, while the county assessor has the neighborhood broken down into several subneighborhoods based on subdivision filing number. These groupings can be combined by the appraiser and the entire neighborhood can then be modeled, if the appraiser determines that it lends credibility to the analysis.

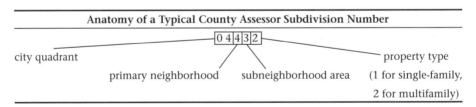

Anatomy of a Typical County Assessor Subdivision Number

|0|4|4|3|2|

city quadrant — primary neighborhood — subneighborhood area — property type (1 for single-family, 2 for multifamily)

If the subneighborhood represents significantly different houses in the same overall neighborhood, then it might be preferable to model the subneighborhoods separately. House style, builder, age of the home, lot size, and other factors can provide the appraiser with indications of the legitimacy of combining subneighborhoods. The best approach, however, may be to simply question a colleague at the county assessor's office about the nature of the neighborhood. Often these mass appraisers have already developed a grouping strategy and are more than willing to discuss this with fee appraisers. Again, the appraiser needs to make this determination prior to the modeling process.

Based on the experience of the authors, the ideal number of sale properties usually ranges between 18 and 32. This range is significantly dependent on the characteristics of the residential market area but provides adequately for the primary elements of comparison. It may be possible to combine separate neighborhoods, treating each area with a unique neighborhood (dichotomous) variable in the model, or by showing similarity through mean or median comparison, and variance and skew comparison.

If the appraiser is faced with many areas that are too small to be modeled separately, then a process called *cluster analysis* can be employed. This type of analysis can be used in areas where the assessor has neighborhoods broken down into very small units. If census information is in the database, census tracts or census blocks can be used. The neighborhoods are grouped based on certain property characteristics, such as the mean age, mean size, or mean value of properties in each neighborhood. The assessor's estimate of market value is a shortcut to grouping the data. For example, if the average age of two neighborhoods was 10 years and the average size was 2,000 square feet of living area, then the average market price according to the county assessor could alert the appraiser to other factors that are significantly different. If one neighborhood has an average assessor's value of $100,000 while another neighborhood has an average assessor's value of $500,000, then the appraiser would probably opt to not combine these two areas.

Cluster analysis can compare an independent variable (property characteristic) to sale price. Cluster analysis can also compare one independent variable to another independent variable. For example, in one neighborhood newer homes could generally be larger while older homes are smaller. Cluster analysis of two independent variables, where the relationship is not immediately obvious, can be highly useful. Within a market area it can help identify the best comparables and estimate the size of adjustments. Similarly, cluster analysis can greatly help in identifying the relevant location variable—i.e., the neighborhood or market area. Cluster analysis may assume that the average age, size, and assessor's value is a good representation of each neighborhood. The best approach appraisers can use is to monitor closely the grouping of neighborhoods carefully. Good judgment, based on experience and specific knowledge of neighborhoods, can also be used to group the data. As with the adjustment process, appraisal principles guide the process.

Step 2. Creating the Sales File

Once the frame is determined, the next step is to create a sales file. This sales file will then be applied to the regression analysis to create the appraisal model.

A sales file can contain any number of sales. Any data outside the frame have been determined by the analyst to have a negligible direct effect on the subject.

The frame should include more (or far more) sales than the appraiser expects to use in the analysis. It can be likened to a "comp search" where all the sales in the market segment form the initial look at the available data. When an appraiser uses the traditional sales comparison approach, the sales collected and analyzed can be considered a manual sales file.

All of the data editing and enhancing (confirming and verifying) required by the scope of the assignment is performed. The verification level that appraisers employ with the sales comparison approach also needs to be undertaken with appraisal modeling. Some of the adjustment considerations, particularly those performed before adjustments for physical factors, may need to be accomplished before the sales file can be analyzed. Conditions of sale, property rights transferred, any significant expenditures undertaken by the grantee immediately after sale, and any related financing terms are factors that could affect the *economic* sale price. A separate "reliability" rating can be created for each sale, reflecting the level of verification, confirming source, and original source.

As with the traditional sales comparison approach, any sale that requires "too much" adjusting may need to be excluded from the appraisal model (given a "zero" reliability rating). The justification must always be that the property is not competitive with the subject—i.e., an economic reason—or that the data are grossly unreliable. The deleted sale and the reasons for the deletion should be disclosed or reported, depending on the level of analysis and reporting the client has requested—e.g., a self-contained report could discuss each deleted comparable, while a summary report might outline the general nature of the market data deletions. Similarly the scope of the appraisal assignment could define the level of detail in the analysis.

Selecting Variables

Once the data are adjusted to economic sale price, the next step is to identify and code certain variables to use in the regression model. This is usually a quick process, but there are important subtleties.

Recall that there are three types of independent variables that the appraiser needs to scrutinize. Primary variables are those that are considered fundamental to the purchase decision, such as income (for an investment property) or living area, bathroom counts, age, and basement area (in the case of the residential example). Secondary variables for housing are property amenities such as air-conditioning, garage type, fireplaces, and swimming pools. For an industrial property, these could include loft area, door height, or office space. Whether a variable is considered a primary or secondary variable can depend on local building characteristics and market demand. Air-conditioning, for example, is considered a secondary variable in Denver, whereas in Phoenix it is a primary variable. In general, a primary variable is one that buyers "must have" in their decision-making matrix. A secondary variable is one that is a "preference" but not required by the buyer.

Note that the overall variable array needs to make appraisal sense. If the appraiser knows that a particular neighborhood borders a golf course and that this location feature significantly affects value, then the appraiser needs to make sure that this variable is included in any appraisal model he or she creates. There are several statistical methods for variable identification that are beyond the scope of this book. The traditional appraiser focus on variables (elements of comparison) is adequate for much production work in typical markets.

Having identified the relevant variables, the appraiser must decide at the outset whether the data set being used has enough variables (or surrogate variables) to allow for meaningful analysis. For example, if a measurement of living area is not consistently or accurately available, then the appraiser may decide that the data are *insufficient* for analysis. If, on the other hand, a secondary variable is unavailable, such as a fireplace, then it may still be possible to perform an adequate appraisal analysis. Sometimes a needed variable such as *quality* is not in the data set—e.g., most MLS listing do not name such a field. However, many MLS forms have a field called *roof type*. In many markets, roof type can be an effective surrogate or substitute for quality. Using a proxy variable takes advantage of the high correlation. In this case, houses with tile roofs correlate highly with construction quality overall, i.e., they are collinear.

"Subjective" Property Characteristics

How about "subjective" characteristics such as condition, functional utility, and view? In general, if something can be observed, it can be measured. The only qualifier is that some things are easier to measure accurately than others.

- Effective age would seem difficult to measure, but it can be broken down into component parts such as roof, kitchen remodel, bath remodel, recarpeting, age of paint, replacement of plumbing, electrical, etc.
- A blended age can consider the age of an add-on, weighted by size, compared to the original structure.
- Construction quality seems difficult but actually starts from a base relative cost relationship, which closely reflects what the market originally paid for it. The base relative cost relationship continues long into the lives of each type of construction.
- View can be broken down into breadth of view, height of view, obstructions and the potential for future obstruction by new construction, and what is viewed.

The *only* constraint is how much effort an appraiser wishes to put into measuring the given element of comparison. A *roof* surrogate is good; personal viewing and rating of observed quality is better. Once measured, on a consistent basis, these variables can be compared and adjusted. Inclusion in a regression equation requires similar effort to be accurate and thorough as does the traditional method but reduces subjective analytical variance. The difference is that the use of all the available data ensures better objectivity and is reproducible and more consistent.

Table 8.1 provides a shortened example of a data file that would usually involve anywhere from 10 to 50 or more relevant sales. Once data are collected and sale conditions are accounted for, the appraiser can create a sales file with valuation variables. This abbreviated example includes both primary and secondary variables.

Table 8.1	Sample Sales File					
Sale	Sale Price	Sale Date	Living Area (Sq. Ft.)	Basement (Sq. Ft.)	Year of Construction	House Style
1	$100,000	Jan-98	2,000	0	1976	Ranch
2	$105,000	May-98	1,800	600	1978	2-Story
3	$110,000	Jun-97	2,300	1,000	1978	2-Story
4	$105,000	Sep-98	1,450	800	1976	Tri-Level
5	$112,000	Nov-97	2,100	750	1977	2-Story

The analyst can determine several things about the arrayed sales immediately. First, the year of construction of the properties in this neighborhood are so similar (ranging from 1976 to 1978) that what may often be a primary variable will probably not be significant in this case. If the model does determine that year of construction is significant, the appraiser needs to make sure that the resulting coefficient values make appraisal sense and that they are not replacing another variable. For example, age in this example could be a stand-in for building style or quality—i.e., one builder built in 1976, while another, poorer-quality builder built in 1978. A good way to check for this is to evaluate the coefficient value. If the age value is negative (i.e., older homes are more valuable), then, for example, there may be older, Victorian-styled homes in the neighborhood that have undergone renovations and remodeling. The appraiser can either model them separately or simply exclude homes beyond a certain year of construction. Regardless, the appraiser needs to know the data well enough that 100-year-old Victorian homes are not included with 25-year-old tract homes. A natural advantage of statistical techniques is that such concepts and comparisons are brought out in the analysis by graphic methods, data exploration, and statistical contrasts, enhancing any advantages of professional experience and competence.

Continuous Variables in Regression

The variables in a regression analysis model need to be continuous (or at least act as such) or a choice (a or b) variable. Recall that in Chapter 3 there were three basic levels of data: nominal, ordinal, and interval. Also, recall that interval-level data carry mathematical meaning. The other two types of data were used to name (nominal) or order (ordinal) data. Continuous variables such as living area, basement area, lot size, age, and market (time) are already interval level. Other variables may be binomial or *multiple choice,* with *each* choice being represented by a yes/no binomial variable. A variable denoting whether a home has a pool or not is a binomial variable, usually represented by a 1 or 0.

House style can be significant in determining property value, but this variable would normally be nominal, simply naming the style of the sale property. How, then, can the appraiser include these housing styles as continuous variables? One approach would be to code house style as follows:

$$Ranch = 1$$
$$Two\text{-}story = 2$$
$$Tri\text{-}level = 3$$

While this coding scheme is a convenient method from an identification perspective, recall that it is still a nominal data array. The numbers used are meant for identification (naming) purposes only. One could very well reverse the coding scheme (with ranch = 3 and tri-level = 1) with the same results. If the appraiser used this coding in the regression model, the computer would take the numbers literally, and based on the coefficient value, tri-level homes would receive three times the value of ranch homes, which is erroneous. These values would be affected by the coding scheme (i.e., what the appraiser decided arbitrarily in terms of coding) rather than the market data itself.

The technically correct method to code nominal level data is to create separate dichotomous (binomial, or yes-no) categorical variables for each house style *less one.* For example, if there were four basic house styles in the neighborhood, then there should be separate variables for *three* of the house styles. The fourth becomes an automatic default "yes" when each of the other three are "no." In other words, the house style *not* selected becomes the "base" variable. The following example illustrates this coding process and the results. In this context, these are called *dummy* variables. Use one less dummy variables than there are choices.

Table 8.2	Coding Process and Resulting Valuation Equation		
Style of Subject Property	Values		
	Variable 1 (Ranch)	Variable 2 (Two-Story)	Variable 3 (Bi-Level)
Ranch	1	0	0
Two-Story	0	1	0
Bi-Level	0	0	1
Tri-Level	0	0	0

Resulting Coefficient Values:
Variable 1 (Ranch) = $5,000
Variable 2 (Two-Story) = $2,500
Variable 3 (Bi-Level) = $3,000

For this very homogeneous neighborhood of otherwise very similar homes, the style element might be the only primary variable needed.

Resulting Valuation Equations:					
	Value	Variable 1	Variable 2	Variable 3	Other Variables
Sale #1 (Ranch)	$105,000 =	($5,000 × 1) +	($2,500 × 0) +	($3,000 × 0) +	$100,000
Sale #2 (Two-Story)	$102,500 =	($5,000 × 0) +	($2,500 × 1) +	($3,000 × 0) +	$100,000
Sale #3 (Bi-Level)	$103,000 =	($5,000 × 0) +	($2,500 × 0) +	($3,000 × 1) +	$100,000
Sale #4 (Tri-Level)	$100,000 =	($5,000 × 0) +	($2,500 × 0) +	($3,000 × 0) +	$100,000

The equations above illustrate how the mechanics work using these dummy variables. The fourth type of house, tri-levels, become the base home in the valuation equation. For simplicity, all of the other valuation factors are included under the last variable category, which in this case could be thought of as including the base house plus lot value. Mechanically, the equations include all of the house style variables, but each sale property receives value for a house style only with one of the variables (or not at all with the case of tri-level houses) because the value zero is used with the other variables.

This scenario works well with other categorical variables, such as fireplaces, garage size (i.e., one car or two cars), basement style, swimming pools, and location factors such as golf course proximity—i.e., any variable that is a choice, whether dichotomous or multiple choice. It can be an alternative way of modeling market conditions (time). The appraiser needs to do this recoding *before* any modeling occurs. The mechanics of this are simple and instantaneous (via computer) once understood. This method can also work for choice dependent variables, say, when two or more locations are used in the model and the appraiser wants the model to test for differences between the location groups. The outcome can be interpreted in the same manner. The indicated location value could be applied to a traditional adjustment model.

In practice, coding of this type is quick to do electronically. Once set up, the computer replaces much of the tedious pondering, comparing, and fitting and justifying required by traditional methods. Statistical modeling allows the appraiser to devote more time to good observation, measurement, and interpretation.

Collinearity

In regression analysis the use of more variables is not always better. One reason is *collinearity* (or multicollinearity). Where one variable is closely related to others, that single variable alone can account for most of the influence of the entire group of independent variables, and that single variable may even give a better estimate alone than together with the other. Remember the example of the collinearity of *roof type* and *overall quality.*

Many statistics students find the multicollinearity concept hard to understand, but it is easy for appraisers, who work with it every day. In residential appraisal, the variables representing square feet of total living area and number of bedrooms are collinear—i.e., a relationship exists between independent variables—as are number of bedrooms and total number of rooms. If two or more variables are correlated in the sample data, then *multi*collinearity is present.

Examples of other variables that often may be so linked include the following:

- Condition versus quality
- Number of bathrooms versus number of plumbing fixtures
- Number of car spaces versus garage size (square feet)

The strong rule of thumb is that if two variables in effect measure the same property characteristic, then one of them should be excluded. Always consult with your data source to determine that you understand the data definition of all of your variables. Watch especially for variables that have a direct mathematical relationship—e.g., total rooms versus bedrooms and other rooms. This creates *perfect* multicollinearity, which is highly undesirable. (Your statistical package will stop.)

For a realistic example, assume that square feet of living area, total bedroom count, and total room count are all included in the sales file. The appraiser needs to select one of these variables as the improvement size variable for the modeling process. Including all three would result in the model either partitioning the valuation effect of improvement size across two or three variables or developing coefficient values that do not make sense for one or more of these variables. (One may even turn out negative.) Conversely, characteristics that clearly impact value should somehow be measured by a variable, whether directly or through a readily available surrogate variable.

Note that there is some trade-off between applying more data and the possible lower quality of that data. This balancing requires appraisal and statistical expertise. The constraint is the cost of analysis, which is a valid consideration. Overall reliability is a consideration in the needs of and in agreement with the client. The Uniform Standards of Professional Appraisal Practice recognizes that there are varying levels of reliability, with the level of a particular assignment decided by the client in consultation with the appraiser. The level of reliability is to be disclosed relative to the scope and extent of the appraisal. It will have been affected by the client, other intended users, and the intended use of the appraisal report.

Choice of Comparables—A Key Difference

In regression analysis, the rules and guidelines governing what constitutes a good array of comparable data are the same as with the traditional sales comparison approach. *What is different is the amount of information extracted from the available market data.* The traditional method discards the least useful data in favor of the most similar comparables, whereas statistical methods squeeze out whatever information there is. The traditional method using four or five comparables discards valuable information. Buried within the available market data is information on

- Reliability estimate
- Market segment size
- Homogeneity of the market
- Market velocity (activity levels, direction, and change)
- Efficiency of the model
- Numerous adjusted pairs

In some markets access to data is limited. Market data may be hidden by participants, hoarded by appraisers, or protected by law. This is common in specialty property types, rural areas, and non-disclosure states. The traditional method of focusing on the few, most relevant sales may be the best in these situations. When data availability is poor (either in quality or quantity), then research, investigation, verification, and authentication become prime tasks of the appraiser. The cost of collecting data is a major factor in the cost of analysis. Clients will not pay for the appraiser's time to ferret out comprehensive detailed information on marginally relevant comparables. In fact, the ability to uncover the best data in a timely fashion is an important element of appraisal expertise, which requires skill and experience.

Yet the traditional approach still limits the analysis to a few comparables in the traditional model when data are available on every sale, in good detail and accuracy, including the relevant elements of comparison. Theoretically, necessary adjustment support can be squeezed from pairs, adjusted pairs, grouped pairs, decision tree, choice-variable regression, or by the use of some other method. But these methods are seldom applied. When good, complete data are available, statistical methods are more reliable because available market data are involved, not discarded.

If the subject property is similar to the sales sample, then the model will provide an estimate of value that can be used with a degree of confidence, dependent on several factors, such as:

- The quality of the data
- The homogeneity of the market area
- The appropriateness of the model
- The number of sales

For example, if the model shows a value of $500 per square foot of living area and the neighborhood is a typical suburban tract subdivision, then the appraiser should check the modeling process carefully. Appraisal experience may tell the appraiser that this $500 amount is too high.

As an example of the application of appraisal theory, suppose the appraiser is modeling a neighborhood that borders a golf course. The sales file contains 25 sales, with only three sales bordering the golf course. The appraiser models the entire neighborhood without distinguishing the three properties bordering the golf course. A better approach could be to identify the golf course as a binomial (0/1) field. Part of the higher sales prices would be now captured by the *golf course* variable. Since the subject would have a 0 in that field, a better value estimate will result. However, there may be an even better model. The appraiser, for example, might exclude those three properties from the analysis and rerun the model. Why? Because those three sales might have collinearity with another important variable. (The original builder could have built only larger homes on the golf course lots.) The results from this new model would represent homes in the neighborhood without the golf course influence corrected for any obvious (or hidden) collinearities. Since plenty of good data are available, a better model results. It is sometimes wise to run the regression both ways, see what happens, and determine the economic reason for the difference. Note that paired sales adjustment in this case would provide an excessive golf course adjustment. Also note that once those data are in the software, naming and rerunning regressions in different ways takes only a matter of seconds. It is faster and provides more clarity for the analyst than the grid method. All that is needed is the data, the software, and an understanding of electronic data analysis.

Step 3. Preliminary Tools for Interpreting Data

The key to surviving the modeling process and not being overwhelmed by the statistical output generated by today's software is to stay focused on the appraisal aspect of the process. Visual output can be a crucial tool. Often a *picture* of the data can be more readily understood than a table of confusing numbers. Many graphic methods are available in statistical software. Two important graphical methods are scatter plots and graphs of sales ratios. These methods are easy to understand, and, more importantly, they allow the appraiser to evaluate the data.

Scatter Plots

Scatter plots are exactly what they sound like—a plot of data that can tell an appraiser whether a sale property "fits" with other data in the sales sample. Such two-dimensional scatter plots are available on all statistical packages and spreadsheet add-ons and on some residential appraisal form and template software packages. Figure 8.1 illustrates a simple scatter plot of sale price and square feet of living area.

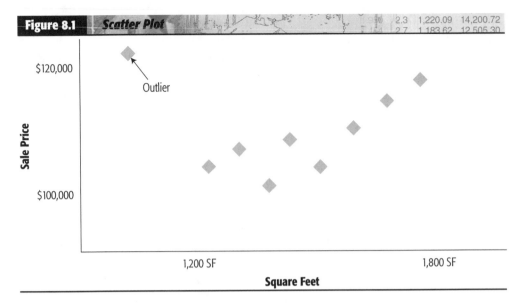

Figure 8.1   Scatter Plot

Examining the scatter plot can tell the analyst several things immediately. First, the sale prices range between $100,000 and approximately $120,000, with a corresponding range of total living area of approximately 1,200 to 1,800 square feet. What if the subject property is 3,000 square feet? What if the subject property's value estimate is $175,000? Generally, caution must be exercised when the subject property lies outside of the range of primary variables such as living area and sale price. While this type of analysis can be gleaned from frequency tables, graphs can present the data in a readily understood format and include two variables.

Another feature is that the graphical presentation such as the scatter plot can often identify obvious outlier cases, i.e., sale properties that lie outside the expected range of a particular variable. For example, the scatter plot in Figure 8.1 has one sale that obviously lies outside both the sale price and living area range of the other sales. The appraiser can run other scatter plots or examine the sales file to determine possible reasons for the aberrant nature of the outlier. It may be a data entry error. Perhaps it is the only sale property that has an oil well. Or perhaps it is the only sale property that sold in 2000 (while the other sales occurred in 1999, after a new, major employer moved in). The appraiser can use this type of graphical analysis to determine if data need to be excluded from the analysis or, more importantly, if there are other factors that must be accounted for in the modeling process. A thorough investigation *takes only seconds* for each pair of variables. Independent variables can be compared to actual sale prices *or to each other*. Hidden relationships jump out and announce themselves.

Sales Ratio Graph

Another important graphical tool concerns the model output after the modeling process takes place. It involves graphing the ratio of estimated value to sale price, which is known as the *sales ratio*:

sales ratio = sale price estimate / actual sale price

The closer this ratio is to 1.0, the more accurate the estimate is. The sales ratio is really useful as an evaluative tool when the appraiser graphs all sales using the sales ratio. With that graph, patterns can be readily checked, using a similar methodology as with scatter plots. Generally, the sales ratios are plotted with the sales ratio along the y-axis and with the independent variable, such as living area, month of sale, age, etc., along the x-axis. The sales ratio should be randomly scattered along the 1.0 latitude of the sales ratio axis.

Consistent patterns may point to interactive effects of one or more variables on the sale price estimate. For example, if a sales ratio graph is performed using month of sale, the appraiser can verify that any sale appreciation has been accounted for. If there is a pattern, then the model needs to be reexamined.

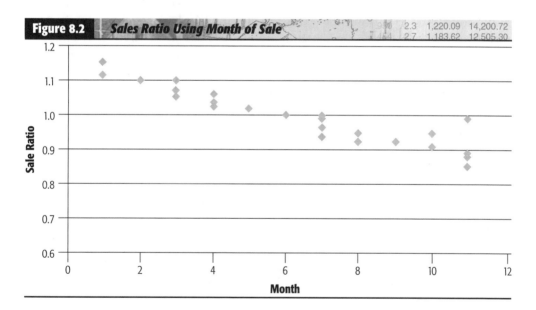

Figure 8.2   *Sales Ratio Using Month of Sale*

Suppose Figure 8.2 were created using month of sale. The sales ratio clearly indicates that there is a consistent overestimation of sale price early in the sale year, while there is a consistent underestimation in the latter part of the year. Faced with this result, the appraiser can return to the modeling coefficients (covered later in this section) and determine first if there is a coefficient for market trends and second, if there is, what the value is. Other tests can be undertaken to check that the model variable makes appraisal sense. Obviously, if the appraiser suspects that the market is appreciating during the sale period and the model indicates that the market trend is either missing or depreciating, then further analysis must be undertaken. Every model can be tested via sales ratio checks for all primary variables, as well as applying the technique to any other variable in the model that the appraiser feels like checking.

Dealing with Problems

Generally, any problems with variables that do not possess consistent sales ratios can be dealt with by reconsidering the variables in the model; in other words, the problem often arises when collinear variables interact, either positively or negatively. It may also arise if an important element of value is omitted—e.g., a significant property tax differential applying to some of the sales and not to others. Another example could be where a good school district is adjacent to another. The *school* variable might be a significant, even primary, factor. At other times, variables should be excluded because they are not statistically significant. The appraiser can insert or delete such variables into the equation to determine if that solves the problem. The variable checks described above can be undertaken whenever there is a question in the modeling process. For example, if a model does not include age, the appraiser still must check this factor using the sales ratio analysis outlined above because all independent variables should be randomly associated with the dependent variable after the analysis is completed. If not, it is incumbent on the appraiser to explain why a relationship not explained by the model is present.

The graphical analyses illustrated in this section are easily accessible through all common statistical software. These methods provide quick, easy checks on model output. There are, of course, statistical checks, which are covered in Step 5.

Step 4. Regression Modeling

Once the sales file data have been edited and the data have been coded for use in the regression model, the regression model is run. The routines recommended here are simple, as statistical procedures go. Whatever statistical package you use, the procedure will be like learning any new software. The appraisal models here will be presented generically so that readers can apply these steps to whatever software packages they choose. The exact process will vary with the software used.

Regression analysis software usually requires the user to distinguish the dependent variable from the independent variables. The appraiser then needs to list all of the independent variables that will be analyzed, including all recoded variables. Again, this can be done very quickly with point-and-click or typed instructions.

Once the data set is selected, the regression model usually requires that you indicate the method of variable selection. Variables can be forced into the model (in a process known as *forward regression* or *backward regression* selection) or they can be entered one at a time (*stepwise regression*). Generally, stepwise selection is recommended. In this method, the variables are entered one at a time with the most significant variable selected first (usually the living area variable or bedroom total variable). The appraiser can then gauge the impact of adding each variable to the model. "Growing" the model in this way helps the analyst understand the relationship and impact of each variable.

How does the regression model know when to stop adding variables to the model? This may be determined by the software, which looks at the contributory value of each new variable. Adding a variable decreases the amount of unexplained variation in the relationship between the dependent variable (sale price) and the independent variables (living area, basement area, age, time, etc.). The model theoretically would add new valuation variables to the model until nearly all of the variation is explained. In this case, the estimates of each sale price would be exactly the same as the actual sale prices—and the R^2 statistic would be 1.00, or 100%. (As previously stated, this never happens.) Most good appraisal models will explain 60% to 80% of the economic relationship between sale price and property characteristics such as living area, basement size, age, market trend, etc. (the R^2 statistic), and have 3% to 7% average errors per sale property (the COD/COV statistics). The automatic variable regression run will usually stop adding variables after the contributory effect falls below a certain threshold.

A stepwise regression model adds variables in the following manner. First, it adds the *best* independent variable, based on the explanatory power of the variable as it relates to sale price.[2] In most cases, this is the living area variable. The regression model then reruns the regression equation with the independent variable, and selects the next best independent variable. It then adds this variable to the model, which is then run again. This cycle is repeated until all of the best variables are included.

What happens if the model finds no significant independent variables to include? Then computing stops. The analyst can then do one of three things:

1. End the modeling process
2. Select a new set of variables.
3. Lower the threshold that allows variables to enter the model. This threshold is usually specified by a *pin* or *pout* value. This value is usually set by the software at 0.05 or 0.10, which can be interpreted as a probability that the variable to be added actually contributes to the model.

Note that most software packages allow the user to change the criteria used by the regression analysis to include or exclude variables. Adjusting these upward will sometimes allow marginal variables to enter the equation. The major pitfall in inserting too many variables is that a variable that does not really contribute to the value of a property will be allowed into the model, and therefore the model will contain an inaccurate coefficient value for that variable.

2.　It is wise to consider using the best variable as the unit of measure–e.g., land value per square foot.

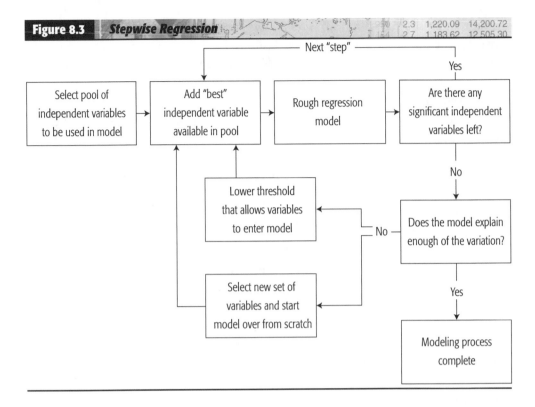

Figure 8.3   Stepwise Regression

Although this scenario is possible, appraisers have one factor in their favor—their experience at estimating value. An appraiser can simply look at the coefficient value and make a determination as to the reasonableness of the model because the coefficients can be evaluated based on their appraisal veracity. For example, if the model returns a coefficient value of $50,000 for a fireplace, the appraiser already knows there is a problem. The chance that a bogus variable value slips through the modeling process without actually contributing to value in the real world is far greater in applications outside of real property appraisal.

Step 5. Output (Verifying)

In addition to R^2 and COD/COV, the other important output step involves using visual tools such as scatter plots and sales ratios. If all of these factors make appraisal sense, then the model can be used as either a supportive tool to the traditional appraising process or as a stand-alone valuation model based on the sales comparison approach.

The important point in verifying the output of *any* appraisal model is that the values for *all* of the valuation variables must make sense. Whether they make sense statistically can be verified with the tools mentioned earlier. Any valuation variable that does not make sense renders the model and its output unusable from an appraisal perspective. The appraiser needs to exclude the bad variable and run the model program again, or the sales file needs to be examined for outlier sales that do not belong with the other sale properties. A third possibility is that the defined neighborhood cannot be modeled effectively using regression analysis—this fact should have been discovered by examining the descriptive data about the neighborhood in the preparation phase of the modeling effort. Then the market area boundaries may need to be revised or similar, competitive neighborhoods added to the pool of market data. (Statistical and graphic tools excel at showing similarity of market segments or neighborhoods.)

Step 6. Reporting Model Results

The final step is the report. If the regression analysis was for the purpose of developing an adjustment factor, then the inclusion of the regression results may need to be presented as with any analysis undertaken in the appraisal process. All important steps need to be presented in a *self-contained* report format so that the user can understand the analysis and conclusions. In a *summary* report format, the steps can be presented in less detail. It is good to clarify assumptions, describe the data, and summarize the procedure.

The case study in the following chapter suggests a format for presenting regression-based output for a subdivision analysis using the sales comparison approach. The appraisal model was comprehensive, in that the model comprised the entire sales comparison approach section of the appraisal report.

Summary

This chapter focused on the "nuts and bolts" of regression modeling using residential real property. The purpose of this chapter was to introduce the mechanics of constructing an appraisal model using linear regression analysis. Points to remember include

1. The importance of identifying the market segment
2. Understanding variable types in the sales file
3. Understanding collinearity and its effects
4. Using visual tools for analysis and in reports
5. Understanding the "art" of regression analysis
6. Understanding the role of the R^2, COD, and COV statistics

Evaluating the model for appraisal veracity is a vital step in the modeling process. The appraiser can and must be the final judge in determining that the output from such models are good indicators of value and not simply interesting mathematical relationships.

Chapter 9 *Case Study*

2.8	1,256.32	11,200.36
2.6	1,450.35	12,315.09
1.9	1,097.06	14,365.25
3.0	1,250.77	11,256.89

This case study is based on an actual valuation of a residential subdivision in northern Colorado.[1] The actual data have been reduced somewhat for ease of presentation. The statistics were calculated using SPSS statistical software. The principles used here apply equally to single home sales. However, this subdivision example extends these methods to another property type, helps focus on the methodology, and shows the universality of the statistical analysis and econometric thinking processes. This example includes a 24-month time trend variable, a continuous size variable, and several binary (0, 1) variables. The method used here is the ordinary least squares (OLS) method. Other (perhaps superior) refinements are available but are left for future, more advanced discussion.

Overview of the Subject Property

The client requested a self-contained report of a complete appraisal on a subdivision located in Fort Collins, Colorado. The subdivision, Rocky Run Phase 2, is a proposed 25-lot subdivision, located east of the city. The average lot price is to be $80,000, with a range of $60,000 to $110,000. Phase 1 had previously sold out, providing a good comparable source because it is very similar to Phase 2. The client, however, wanted the appraiser to include other subdivisions in the area, and the appraiser agreed that they are in the relevant market area and should be included in the frame. Three other subdivisions are located in the market area of the subject property that contains potential comparable lot sales. The client wished to have the appraisers value the land as proposed, with full approvals and infrastructure in place.

---

1. For confidentiality, the appraisers have used different names and descriptions for the subject property and the comparable properties.

The client provided the appraiser with a description of the 25 lots. Ten of the lots were to be situated around the lake located in the interior of the subdivision. Other lots had walk-out grades, some backed onto open space, while some had unobstructed views of the Rocky Mountains. To make it easier to analyze the lot descriptions, the appraisers constructed a table describing each lot group (Table 9.1).

Table 9.1	Lot Group Grid						
Lot Numbers	Group	Average Lot Price	Average Lot Size (Acres)	Lake Frontage	West Views	Open Space	Walk-out
1 through 5	A	$105,000	1.5	Yes	Yes	No	Yes
6 through 10	B	$100,000	1.25	Yes	No	No	No
11 through 15	C	$90,000	1.5	No	No	Yes	Yes
16 through 20	D	$95,000	1.25	No	Yes	Yes	No
21 through 25	E	$90,000	1.0	No	No	No	No

Describing the Sales Data

After examining the comparable subdivisions for comparable lot sales, the appraisers collected and verified information on 60 comparable lot sales. The appraisers drove by each lot and observed if each lot had any water frontage, westerly views, open space, or walk-out grades. Table 9.2 shows the descriptive information collected on the sales data.

Table 9.2	Sales Data Grid					
Subdivision	Average Sale Price	Number of Sales	Lake Frontage	West Views	Open Space	Walk-out
Mountain View	$75,000	12	6 = Yes 6 = No	10 = Yes 2 = No	12 = No	12 = No
Rocky Run Phase 1	$105,000	15	15 = No	9 = Yes 6 = No	8 = Yes 7 = No	7 = Yes 8 = No
Meadow Wood	$90,000	16	16 = No	8 = Yes 8 = No	10 = Yes 6 = No	16 = No
Monte Claude	$100,000	17	10 = Yes 7 = No	8 = Yes 9 = No	17 = No	6 = Yes 11 = No
Total		60	16 = Yes 44 = No	35 = Yes 25 = No	18 = Yes 42 = No	13 = Yes 47 = No

There were enough hits on each of the identified variables to include them in the regression model. Note that the appraisers examined the total number of hits for the entire sales file, not individual subdivisions. Location was one of the variables to be examined and was treated as another lot characteristic. The following conclusions and decisions were made and stated clearly in the appraisal report:

1. All of the subdivisions had basically the same amenities such as home owners fees, common areas, paved roads, water availability, sewer and utility taps, etc. Were this not the case, the appraisers would have to consider whether the design of this analysis was sufficient to account for any such differences.
2. Lot sizes ranged from an average of 0.5 acres in the Mountain View subdivision to 1.6 acres in the Monte Claude subdivision. The appraisers decided to include a lot size variable in the model.
3. The maximum sales period was defined to be the two years prior to the effective date of the appraisal. A market trend variable, coded backwards from 1 to 24 (i.e., 1 month ago, 2 months ago, etc.), was applied.
4. The first three subdivisions were each assigned a variable that identified whether a lot was in that particular subdivision. The coding scheme was 0 = not in the subdivision, 1 = in the subdivision. Because of its similarity to the subject property (Phase 2), Rocky Run Phase 1 was not coded and conveniently becomes the fourth reference subdivision.

After the sales file was coded, the appraisers contacted the county and at least one of the parties involved with each transaction to verify that each sale was an arm's-length transaction with no unusual conditions or financing that would have affected the sale price.

Modeling Process

Next, the appraisers decided on the following model equation, based on the stated assumptions:

Dependent variable = Lot value (what we want to predict)
Independent variable 1 = Market trend (coded 1 to 24)
Independent variable 2 = Lot size (in square feet)
Independent variable 3 = Lake frontage (1 = yes, 0 = no)
Independent variable 4 = West views (1 = yes, 0 = no)
Independent variable 5 = Open space (1 = yes, 0 = no)
Independent variable 6 = Walk-out (1 = yes, 0 = no)
Independent variable 7 = Located in Mountain View (1 = yes, 0 = no)
Independent variable 8 = Located in Meadow Wood (1 = yes, 0 = no)
Independent variable 9 = Located in Monte Claude (1 = yes, 0 = no)

Note that most of the variables in the equation are coded as dichotomous variables (0, 1). This allows binary variables to be included, as well as the *three* subdivision dummy variables to identify *four* subdivisions. Which variables would be considered primary variables? Perhaps all of them, given that these characteristics are generally considered to be important by agents, buyers, and sellers who were interviewed for verification.

First, the appraisers enter these sale properties into an Excel spreadsheet. Then the file is transferred to an SPSS file for preliminary analysis. Frequency statistics are run on the sale prices for every sale to confirm that there are no troublesome outlier sales. The same test is performed on the lot sizes, and the coding used for the market trend variable is checked to ensure that there are no errors and that the months ranged from 1 to 24, rounded to the nearest month. Variables 3 through 6 are checked for correct coding also.

Next the appraisers set up the regression equation parameters—a simple naming step that varies. The appraisers specify the dependent and independent variables, the type of regression (multiple linear regression), how the variables would be entered into the model (stepwise selection), and the type of output. This last specification refers to the kind of plotting the computer generates and any additional output variables, such as the estimated sale price for each sale property. Standard output generally includes output statistics such as R^2, standard error of the estimate (the average difference between the estimated sale price and the actual sale price for the sale properties), the coefficients used and not used, the coefficient values, and the F-value, which will be explained later.

Typical Output

The output in Figure 9.1 is typical for most software packages, although the actual presentation may differ between packages:

Figure 9.1	Output Example				
Variable Entered on Step Number 9 . . .			Open space		
Multiple R^2			0.91792		
R^2			0.84257		
Adjusted R^2			0.82393		
Standard Error			7039.69130		
Variables in the Equation					
Variable	**B**	**SE B**	**Beta (β)**	**t**	**Sig t**
Mountain View	-12099.4494	6322.1617	-0.275279	-1.914	0.0594
Meadow Wood	-5726.21412	3174.2762	-0.105091	-1.804	0.0752
Monte Claude	4862.239510	3579.2371	0.074266	1.358	0.1783
Open space	2471.552146	2205.6196	0.072798	1.121	0.2660
Sale date	624.875851	200.1863	0.169689	3.121	0.0025
Lot size	10616.12061	3473.6575	0.424968	3.056	0.0031
Walk-out	-5783.23777	2201.6773	-0.162529	-2.627	0.0104
West view	7336.254682	2037.9469	0.216085	3.600	0.0006
Lake frontage	32761.81143	2850.8425	0.869429	11.492	0.0000
(Constant)	54817.83573	4512.9905		12.147	0.0000

The output in Figure 9.1 contains important information about the regression model used in this analysis. Note that most statistical packages provide much more output than most analysts will find useful. For most applications, and for learning purposes, focus on one statistic at a time. Interpreting output statistics of an appraisal valuation model requires a combination of valuation expertise and statistical understanding. Figure 9.1 provides numbers that describe precisely what appraisers formerly considered part of the "art."

R^2

The R^2 statistic is 0.84257, which is a more-than-acceptable result (remember that the general rule of thumb is 0.60 or above). In other words, over 84% of the total variation in the sales data is explained by this model, while the remaining 16% is not explained. The unexplained portion may be a variable that was left out, measurement error, or a plain random factor within the "negotiation range" of buyers and sellers. The adjusted R^2 statistic of 0.82393 may be a better measurement of the model's explanatory power because it takes into account the effects of using "too many" variables.

Standard Error of the Regression

The next output item to focus on is the standard error term of 7039.69. This means that a sale estimate will vary from its actual value by $7,039 on average. This number alone is meaningless unless related to the average sale price in the sale sample. Assuming the average sale price is approximately $95,000, then dividing the standard error by the average sale price would yield a 7.4% value—essentially the coefficient of variation, which measures the average error in percentage terms. This result is also within the rule of thumb of COV of less than 10%.

$$COV = (7039.69 / 95,000) \times 100 = 7.4\%$$

Variable Names

The first column of the regression output details the calculated coefficients. In the table of output, the first column lists the variable names used in the analysis. Keeping the variable names as close to actual meaning as possible is advisable. Using cryptic variable labels can make interpretation of the output difficult for the appraiser, let alone for the user of the report.

Coefficients

The second column refers to the actual coefficient values that will be used in the appraisal model's valuation equation. Generally these totals can be rounded to eliminate the decimal places. Often appraisers round these to the nearest 10th or 100th place. Remember that these coefficients may be different from typical values used in adjustment grids.

Standard Error of Coefficient

The third column refers to the standard error of each coefficient, which can be distinguished from the standard error of the regression as explained above. The standard error, like the standard deviation, indicates the expected deviation from the true value of the variable but applies to the *sample* rather than the whole population of lots. Obviously, the narrowest possible deviation is desired. The deviation spread can also affect the *t*-value (covered below). For example, the open space variable has a relatively large deviation (2,205) when compared to its coefficient value (2,472); it is so large that when one constructs a confidence interval for this variable, defined as $2,471 \pm (1.96 \times 2,205)$, the lower bound is negative.

$$2,471 + (1.96 \times 2,205) = 2,471 + 4,321.8 = 6,792.8$$

$$2,471 - (1.96 \times 2,205) = 2,471 - 4,321.8 = -1,850.8$$

This means that the number zero would be included in the 95% confidence interval, which in turn means that the true coefficient value may in fact be zero. Generally, the more unstable or uncertain a variable is in relation to the dependent variable, the greater the standard error relative to the coefficient value.

Beta

Column 4 refers to the Beta (β) value, which indicates the partial correlation of the variable and is used in stepwise regression in deciding which variable to add next. Its interpretation and usefulness is beyond the scope of this book, but any standard book on regression will explain its use and practicality.

Significance of Variables (*t*-test and *p*-value)

The last two columns in the output refer to the individual significance of each independent variable in the regression equation (another test for significance, the *F*-test, refers to the significance of the overall regression relationship between the dependent variable and all the independent variables). The *t*-test is calculated by dividing the coefficient value by the standard error of that value for an individual variable. For the first variable, Mountain View, the *t*-value is calculated by dividing -12,099.4494 by 6,322.1617, to arrive at a value of -1.914.

$$t = \text{coefficient value} / \text{standard error} = -12,099.4494 / 6,322.1617 = -1.914$$

The statistical program compares this value with the value derived from the model's *t*-distribution to arrive at a significance value, often termed the *p-value*, which ranges from 0.0 to 1.0. This refers to the probability that the relationship between the dependent variable and the independent variable is due to random chance. The number should be as small as possible, although there is no hard-and-fast rule as to what the *p*-value should be. In a manner of speaking, the *p*-value and *t*-value are obverse ways of looking at statistical significance.

In most regression software programs, the user can set the *p*-value tolerance, which would exclude any variable with a *p*-value greater than a set amount. In the example above, the *p*-value tolerance was set to 0.30; if that threshold tolerance had been set lower, say to 0.20, then the open space variable would have been excluded from the model. As it stands, this particular variable is the least reliable in the model equation, which is important to determine so that the appraiser can decide if variables should or should not be included. In this instance, the lot sizes tend to be large, and backing onto an open space area may not be as important to a buyer as other factors. The key fact here is that statistical significance does *not* mean economic importance. Only the coefficient (the adjustment factor) indicates value importance. Recall that our overall approach was to determine the market factors that contribute to value; the variable output above can give the appraiser the analytical framework to present the elements of the market for this particular area.

A closer look at tolerance. Before the model output that was presented in the appraisal report is described, the reasoning behind the use of such a high *p*-value threshold should be examined briefly. In most textbooks, *p*-values are set at 0.05 or 0.10, where a 5% or 10% possibility that the relationship under scrutiny is in fact due to random chance is acceptable. In fact, the thresholds should be set by the circumstances regarding the analysis. For example, when biostatisticians examine certain diagnostic procedures for fatal diseases like AIDS or cancer, the cost (to the patient) of being incorrectly diagnosed can literally be fatal. The threshold tolerances in those types of procedures, and the statistical analysis that verifies these procedures, are set far below 5% or 10%. The same is often true in tolerance limits for items such as aircraft, weapons, toxic substances, or any instance where the cost of being wrong can be catastrophic.

Another reason for rigorous tolerances is due to uncertainty. In psychology, for example, researchers are often faced with describing and analyzing phenomena where there is a significant degree that is not known, so any model that attempted to explain or predict those behaviors would require a wide range of tolerance. In terms of appraisal, the phenomena under question are related to the activity that determines real estate value. This activity is expressed often in interval-level data (the sale price of a property) and involves known factors that contribute to value. Given the degree of certainty that is involved with real estate activity, the tolerances can generally be set to a higher (looser) level. Coefficient values, and their relationship with one another, can be evaluated by appraisers applying economic theory in the context of market experience. The indicated relationship is often previously known or bounded by other methods of estimation. Again, the economic context and appraisal theory circumscribe the equation. The authors often use a threshold limit of 0.30, as in this example.

Simple steps. Rerunning a regression model when adding or subtracting variables is quick and easy. With most software programs, the following general scheme should direct the modeling process:

1. Run the regression analysis with all appropriate variables in the equation.
2. Carefully examine the variable coefficients for their appraisal appropriateness.
3. Exclude those variables that are very iffy (based on low significance).
4. Exclude those variables that have very small relative coefficient values.
5. Reexamine the data or the model for out-of-range coefficients. (Remember that collinear variables may need to be considered together. One may even be the wrong sign but reasonable when grouped with a collinear variable—e.g., total rooms and square feet.)
6. Rerun the regression analysis as often as necessary, repeating steps 2-5 before each regression run.

Remember that there is no "perfect" regression. What is important is your analysis, i.e., what you learn from what the data tell you.

One note on stepwise regression output. In stepwise regression the appraiser can actually follow the building of the valuation equation; at every step, as another variable is added to the model, the regression analysis is rerun, with new statistics generated. Note that the R^2 and standard error terms will improve at each step. The process stops when the t-value tolerance limit (p-value set to some level such as 0.30) or the overall F-value reaches its maximum amount (recall that the F-value increases as variables are added to the regression run). The stepwise process can give clues as to how the regression model was built by the computer. The analyst, then, can redirect the construction of the model as needed.

Constant

The last variable listed on the coefficient table is not really a variable at all. Known as the *constant,* this term is often difficult to explain to non-statisticians. Mathematically, the constant is simply the intercept of the regression line where all of the independent variables are zero. You can conceptualize the constant as the inherent land value as in the cost approach, but this is not strictly correct in statistical terms. Any real interpretation of the constant depends on what exactly is being modeled, which would require discussion of considerations that are beyond the scope of this book. In this example, note that with the dummy variable coding of the subdivision locations *each* has a different constant based on adding the subdivision coefficient values to the constant.

What constitutes a constant value that is "way out of line?" One that is so large that the coefficient values (one or more of them) are affected adversely, becoming unreasonable from an appraisal perspective. The data or the model needs to be reevaluated.

Output Results and Testing

Because the estimated value for each of the 60 sale lots was saved as part of the regression process, the authors created a sales ratio variable by dividing the estimated sale price by the actual sale price for every sale property. An average ratio of 1.0 was achieved for each variable in the equation, although the standard deviation around this average varied by each variable. The important verification at this point concerned the dispersion, measured by the standard deviation, for each independent variable.

Deriving a Valuation Equation from the Model

Once the regression analysis is finalized, the last analytical step is to present the valuation equation, based on the above regression coefficients. This equation is then used to derive the value of the subject parcel, based on individual lot characteristics. This is the same as applying adjustment factors supported by traditional methods. Figure 9.2 illustrates the model equation, with coefficient values rounded.

Figure 9.2	Model Equation			
Coefficient	**Measure**	**Variable**	**Explanation**	
$54,818	Constant			
+ 625	Month	Market trend		
+ 2,472	(0,1)	Open space	(0 = no, 1 = yes)	
+ 10,616	Acres	Lot size in acres		
− 5,783	(0,1)	Walk-out	(0 = no, 1 = yes)	
+ 7,336	(0,1)	Western view	(0 = no, 1 = yes)	
+ 32,762	(0,1)	Lake frontage	(0 = no, 1 = yes)	
− 12,099	(0,1)	Subdivision #1	(0 = no, 1 = yes)	
− 5,726	(0,1)	Subdivision #2	(0 = no, 1 = yes)	
+ 4,862	(0,1)	Subdivision #3	(0 = no, 1 = yes)	
Lot value				

			Lot Category		
Coefficient	**A**	**B**	**C**	**D**	**E**
Constant	$54,818	$54,818	$54,818	$54,818	$54,818
Open space	$0	$0	+ $2,472	+ $2,472	$0
Lot size*	+ $15,924	+ $13,270	+ $15,924	+ $13,270	+ $10,616
Walk-out	− $5,783	$0	− $5,783	$0	$0
West view	+ $7,336	$0	+ $7,336	$0	$0
Lake frontage	+ $32,762	+ $32,762	$0	$0	$0
Total	$105,057	$100,850	$74,767	$70,560	$65,434

*   The average lot size for each lot category was used.

The above equation includes variables based on the property characteristics of the subject property. The subdivision variables, therefore, were not necessary (zero coefficient) to value the lots in the subdivision. The market trend variable also was not necessary (zero coefficient), since the effective date of the appraisal was the end of the sales period used in the analysis. Note that each of the 25 lots in the subject property could have been valued individually using the equation grid in Figure 9.2; the groupings were created to expedite the presentation.

Reporting the Results

This appraisal model result is reported in the following format and makes up the sales comparison approach section of the report. The process of reporting such findings should follow these guidelines:

1. The lot categories used in the analysis are described in detail.
2. Next, an overview of the analytical steps that are undertaken is provided.
3. Each of the subdivisions are described in detail, with the number of lots that are used in the analysis described.
4. Next, a step-by-step description of the analytical steps, including a description of the sales file, the variables examined, and the basic valuation equation, is given.
5. The results of the regression model are then presented, with a description of the regression runs attempted and run.
6. The results of the model are applied to the subject property, using the described lot categories.

The use of graphics and tables can help explain the process in a concise, understandable format. Caution must always be exercised to explain the process and the arrival of the valuation conclusion of the report, depending on the type of report.

2.8	1,256.32	11,200.36
2.6	1,450.35	12,315.09
1.9	1,097.06	14,365.25
3.0	1,250.77	11,256.89

absolute deviation

The difference between an observation and the measure of central tendency (such as the arithmetic mean) for that array, without regard as to the sign (positive or negative) of the difference. For example, if the observed value is 6 and the mean of these observations is 10, then the difference (or deviation) would be 6 – 10 or -4; dropping the negative sign would yield the absolute deviation, which in this case would be 4.

actual value

The term used by assessors to identify the market value of the property derived by examining sales data for a specified period. Generally, the actual value is as of a specified date, based on a preceding sale period (usually 18 to 24 months). The *assessed value* is a value set on real and personal property for the basis of levying taxes. The assessed value may or may not be equivalent to market value, based on issues such as fractional assessments, partial exemptions, and decisions by the assessor to override the market value. *Appraisers are cautioned to fully understand the methodology of a particular jurisdiction before presenting and using either value in their analyses.*

ad valorem property tax

A tax levied in proportion to the value of the real or personal property. *Ad valorem* literally means "according to value."

ANOVA (analysis of variance)

Generally, just a two-variable regression. This is a well-developed body of techniques for analyzing and comparing data without the use of multiple regression. It is particularly useful for testing and comparing group mean scores and variances and for integrating categorical and continuous variables in an analysis. Considered outdated by some, it is well-suited for many appraisal applications building on the underlying economic and appraisal theory, and it is a good pedagogical tool. It can be especially useful in estimating transaction adjustments, sale conditions (motivation), market conditions (time), and space (location). The concepts underlie visual graphic analysis.

array

A set of data identifying some phenomenon. A set of sale properties would include an array of sale prices as well as other arrays pertaining to property attributes.

artificial intelligence

Machine "thinking."

assessed value

See definition of *actual value.*

attribute

A characteristic of a person, thing, or event. In appraising, an element of comparison.

average deviation

The arithmetic mean of the absolute deviations of a set of numbers from a measure of central tendency, such as the median. Used to calculate the coefficient of dispersion.

AVM

Appraisal valuation model or automated valuation model. Both terms refer to electronic algorithm-assisted valuation decision making.

base-home approach

A method of appraising single-family residential properties whereby each residence to be appraised is compared with one having common or typical characteristics and of known value, called the *base home.* The differences between the two in terms of attributes such as size, functional utility, condition, and other factors are weighted by the appraiser to derive the subject property's valuation conclusion. This approach forms the basic construct for multiple regression valuation methodology used in appraisal valuation modeling.

bias

A statistic is biased if it systematically differs from the population parameter being estimated, such as the average sale price. An example in appraisal valuation modeling would be if the model results consistently overvalued properties that sold above the average sale price and undervalued properties that sold below the average sale price.

CAMA (computer-assisted mass appraisal)

A system of appraising property, usually only certain types of real property, that incorporates computer-supported statistical analyses such as multiple regression analysis and adaptive estimation procedures to assist the appraiser in estimating value.

categorical variable

A variable that assigns data based on group identification. The group identification can be ranked or simply be an identifying group label. The power of statistical comparison is limited because the information provided by the categorization is limited. The data values are termed *discrete,* in that there are no values between each data category.

central tendency

The result of data clustering about a value or values. In a normal distribution, the central tendency is constant when measured by the mean, median, or mode. These three statistics are termed *measures of central tendency.*

cluster analysis

Generally, graphing the data points with one variable on one axis and another on the other axis. Can be extended to three-dimensional (fixed-view or real-time) visual analysis on statistical graphing software.

COD (coefficient of dispersion)

The average deviation of a group of numbers from the median expressed as a percentage of the median. In ratio studies, the average percentage deviation from the median ratio. This statistic can be effective as a measure of accuracy in regression modeling small data sets (less than 25 sales).

coefficient (in a regression)

The multiplier applied to the variable. (Analogous to an adjustment factor, such as $54 per square foot. The *$54* is the coefficient; the *square foot* is the independent variable.)

coefficient of determination

The square of the correlation coefficient. Also, a term identifying the R^2 statistic, which is used to evaluate regression models. This statistic measures the amount of total variation explained by the regression model; its utility when estimating point values, such as with appraisal valuation models, is perhaps less useful than statistics that measure the average error, such as the COV or COD. More recent statistical references are dropping this moniker in favor of using the term R^2 directly to identify this statistic. It also avoids confusion with other statistical tools that use the term *coefficient,* such as the coefficient of dispersion or the coefficient of variation.

coefficient of variation (COV)

1. A measure of *relative variation.* It is given by the ratio of the standard deviation of a set of data to the mean of that set of data. This is a way of normalizing the statistic so that it can be compared across all data sets.

2. A standard statistical measure of the relative dispersion of the sample data about the mean of the data; the standard deviation expressed as a percentage of the mean. In regression modeling, this statistic can be estimated by dividing the standard error of the estimate by the average sale price of the sales data set.

collinearity

Correlation between two independent variables in a regression. (Same as *multicollinearity,* if more than two variables are involved.)

continuous variable

A variable that can never be measured exactly. Examples include living area, improved area, and age. Examples of non-continuous data include the number of fireplaces, bedrooms, and bathrooms. It is sometimes useful to group continuous data into discrete groupings, such as grouping single-family residences into living area groups of 1,000-1,500 square feet, 1,501-2,000 square feet, and over 2,000 square feet.

correlation

1. Association between two variables or a measure of such association.

2. A statistical phenomenon where an identified phenomenon implies a corresponding result in another phenomenon. One example would be the size of a property affecting the sale price. In most instances (and controlling for other important factors), the larger a property would garner a greater sale price. This type of correlation between property size and sale price can be measured and evaluated. For example, it may involve a partial correlation, where the relationship is less clear; this often occurs due to other factors affecting the dependent variable.

data

Groups of observations; either qualitative or quantitative.

data set

Refers to a sample of data used in a statistical analysis such as regression modeling. An appraisal example would be the sales file used in an appraisal valuation model.

dependent variable

The variable that may be or is believed to be predicted by or caused by independent variables; response variable; explained variable.

descriptive statistic

A statistic (number) used to describe a data set. (See *inferential statistic.*)

deterministic

Certain, as opposed to probabilistic.

deviation

The amount an individual observation differs (i.e., deviates) from the mean.

discrete data

Data that are categorized into two or more groups. Examples include number of bedrooms, fireplaces, garage spaces, and bathrooms. Discrete data that belongs to only two groups, such as swimming pools (0 = no, 1 = yes), are termed *binary data*. The type of data determines what type of statistical tests can be performed on the data set. Discrete data can sometimes be treated as continuous data for mathematical analysis.

discrete variable

Nominal and ordinal variables are discrete, in that the numeric identification for each is a discrete total and does not include any inherent information about the magnitude of differences between each group.

dispersion

A generic word for "spread." See *standard deviation, standard error,* and *interquartile range.*

disturbance

The "error" or stochastic part of the analysis. It is the way of facing the reality that economic data are not deterministic and will not provide exact answers.

dummy variable

A variable that takes only two positions. Also called *dichotomous, binary,* or *indicator.* If the dependent variable is the dummy, it is often called a *choice* model.

econometrics

The application of mathematical and statistical techniques to economic situations. It can be considered the "scientific" approach to valuation. Its primary importance in the appraisal context is that it accommodates the analysis of electronically delivered market data from a comprehensive database. Traditional methods can be considered more the "art" of appraising, well-suited to difficult-to-obtain, difficult-to-verify market information.

empirical

Using scientific evidence from the real world (i.e., using mathematics and statistics instead of language-based arguments for research and analysis).

error

The unexplained or stochastic part of the analysis. A *measurement* of how "wrong" the value might be. It is the way of facing the reality that economic data are not deterministic and will not provide exact answers.

expert system

Machine trained by a human.

factor

A variable used to identify a property attribute *or* the underlying characteristic of a property that may indirectly affect value *or* the reciprocal of a rate (multiplying net income by the appropriate factor will yield the same result as dividing the same net income by the direct capitalization rate).

function

A mathematical relationship.

functional form

The mathematical function used to model an economic relationship (linear, logarithmic, exponential, piecewise, inverse, among many others).

fuzzy systems

A system that accommodates uncertainty or probability.

game theory

Strategy versus strategy. Buyer and seller negotiations analysis, as opposed to general equilibrium analysis solutions for value estimates.

graphical analysis

Using graphs, charts, and tables to "see" data and thereby uncover relationships, analyze effects, and assist in interpretation.

graphical presentation

Using graphs, charts, and tables in reports to help the reader see the data and to support, explain, and justify interpretations of that data.

hedonic regression

A multivariate analysis that analyzes a compound good, such as a house, that provides several functions in varying proportions.

heuristic

Instructive or pedagogical, exploratory, trial-and-error, rule-of-thumb methodology. More akin to the "art" of appraising.

IAAO

International Association of Assessing Officers, which is the overseeing authority for the nation's assessors. It functions much the same way as the Appraisal Institute.

inferential statistic

A statistic used to infer results based on a relatively small set of data onto a larger set. This type of analysis goes one step beyond simply describing phenomena by attempting to predict outcomes or relationships.

information

Any data that throw light on the estimated parameter, measured by the "Fisher Information number." As the number increases, the variance of the estimate decreases (reliability increases).

information technology

The broad discipline of data gathering, analysis, and interpretation, generally in the electronic, computerized software domain (process technology); utilizing product technologies (hardware).

instrumental variable

A variable that can function as a proxy for something unmeasured or even unmeasurable. Sometimes called a *surrogate variable*.

intercept

In regression analysis, this is the value of the dependent variable when the independent variables are set to zero. In property valuation models, it is often tempting to define the intercept as the inherent land value of a property without any improvements, but this is not the case because the linear relationship may not hold between the data set and the Y-axis. The appraiser should consider the intercept an artifact of the regression equation, rather than a land attribute in the appraisal model.

interquartile range

A measure of spread. It measures the "distance" between the values one-quarter and three-quarters of the way along a data set.

interval variable

A variable based on the actual numeric value of the data itself. For example, the variable Sale Price contains all of the attributes of nominal and ordinal data, but it also possesses meaning in terms of the differences between values. A property that sells for $100,000 has twice the market value of a property that sells for $50,000.

mass appraisal

The process of valuing a set of properties, using a single effective date, a retrospective sales period, common data elements and definitions, and statistical analysis to evaluate the outcome.

mean (greek letter μ, pronounced mü, "mew")

The sum of *n* numbers divided by *n*.

median

The middle-most value in a vector of values—e.g, 7, out of {1, 4, 6, 6, 7, 9, 11, 22, 41}.

mode

The value that occurs most often—e.g., 8, out of {2, 4, 5, 6, 6, 7, 7, 8, 8, 8, 8, 10, 12}.

model

1. A representation that attempts to explain in as great detail as possible the relationship between a dependent variable, such as sale price, and independent variables that reflect factors of supply and demand.

2. A copy or representation that describes the underlying logical structure, mathematical relationships, and the behavior of the agents in the system (buyers, sellers, agents, lenders, and regulators). It can be a single-equation model with one or more independent variables, or it can be a system of equations. It deals with the *purely logical aspects* of valuation theory (as differentiated from the application of real data, empirical testing of the appraisal theory, and interpretation of the results).

multicollinearity

Correlation between three or more independent variables in a regression (same as *collinearity,* if two variables are involved).

neural network

Feedback-sensing, self-training of a machine.

nominal variable

A variable used for group identification, such as house style or neighborhood. This type of data variable is often used in descriptive analysis, although it also has limited applications in inferential analysis.

nonprobability sample

A sample not produced by a scientific random process; for example, it may be a sample based upon an appraiser's *judgment* about which cases to select. It is well-suited for some poorly developed data sets.

observation

The words or numbers that represent an attribute for a particular case.

ordinal variable

A variable based on a ranked order of data, such as a measurement of quality of construction based on a scale of 1 through 5. This type of variable provides more information than nominal data, although it is more limited than interval variables, since the rankings themselves do not provide any information concerning the distance between each ranking. In other words, a ranking variable for quality does not imply that a score of 4 is "twice as good" as a score of 2; the correct interpretation would be that the score of 4 is two levels above the score of 2.

outlier

An observation that is extreme, in that it is out of the typical range. It is usually a *suspect* of error or economic inappropriateness and demands individual attention. Outliers can unduly influence the result of the regression model. The further an observation is from the measures of central tendency, the greater the influence may be.

parcel identifier

The coding used by the assessor's office to identify the location of the property. The identifier may include a hierarchical series of numbers that include the map area, neighborhood, block, and lot or any other identification based on location.

precision

The degree of refinement in the performance of a model. Precision relates to the quality of the model, as opposed to the term *validity,* which relates to the result of the analysis. The precision of an appraisal model would include the types and quality of the variables and data used. The accuracy of the same model would refer to the overall architecture of the model; that is, does the model measure what it purports to measure?

qualitative data

Data that are based on subjective measures, where the data tend to fall into nominal or ordinal categories; *usually represented in the form of words* (see *quantitative data*). An amenity such as View may indeed affect market value but is nevertheless difficult to measure and quantify. Quantitative data, on the other hand, are more objective, in that they are based on interval data that can be measured and compared with much more precision. Qualitative data are still valuable as a source of information, and when correctly ranked or systematically treated, they can significantly improve the appraisal modeling process.

quantitative data

Data in the form of numbers. (Note: qualitative data can often be quantified in the econometric context.)

R^2

See *coefficient of determination.*

random

A number or value that can take on one of several specific possible values. It is not indeterminate but is usually connected with a probability of taking on that value.

rational expectations

The assumption of consistent rational behavior.

regression analysis

A method for determining the association between two or more variables.

reliability

Freedom from random error. Statistically, this relates to the consistency, unbiasedness, and efficiency of a model. Economically, in terms of valuation practice, this may include a rating of the truthfulness and bias of a data source, measurement and transmission error or bias, and verification breadth, depth, and detail. In the future, the analysis of reliability will be as important as the value estimate and will be inseparable from scientific analysis.

risk

The odds or probability of an unfavorable outcome. (See *reliability.*)

robust

The quality of a statistic that is useful in spite of the violations of one of its basic assumptions.

sales ratio

The ratio of the estimated sale price divided by the actual sale price. This is a powerful tool that can be graphically displayed to determine the accuracy of a model in terms of relating the dependent variable (sale price) by a set of independent variables (such as property attributes). It can also be used to evaluate whether there are systematic biases present in the model output.

sample

Any data taken to represent a larger population of data. There are judgment samples, random samples, probability samples, self-selecting samples, etc. A random sample is more akin to the *science* of appraising, while a judgment sample is more akin to the *art* of appraising. Each has its place.

skewed

A distribution that is not symmetrical.

standard deviation

The square root of the variance; the square root of the sum of the deviations squared.

standard error (S.E.)

Exactly the same as standard deviation, except that it applies to a sample rather than to the population.

stochastic

Probabilistic (as opposed to deterministic).

transformation

A mathematical procedure for converting a distribution of data into a more manageable form, such as the transformation of *logistic* relationship into a linear one. Transformation enables linear regression on a non-linear relationship.

truncation

1. Unsupported disregard of available data.
2. Data cut-off, for a non-economic reason—for example, sales occurring after the report date.

variable

A logical collection of attributes. For example, each possible size of a house is an attribute; the collection of all such attributes is the variable Square Feet. (See *random*.)